Rib Baskets

Jean Turner Finley

P9-BZJ-968

Schiffer Publishing Ltd

CREDITS

Proof: Patricia Turner

Photography: Lyn Kelley
Richard McCloskey
Scott Finley

Editing: Lyn Kelley

Special help: Mark Finley
Robert Finley
Jill Ruscheinski
Eugene Turner

Title page:
Above: 7" Key Basket with 1/8" weavers. Below: 10" Melon
Basket with blue dyed flat reed in god's eye and blue round
reed on sides. The "X" design on handle and sides is cane.
10" Egg Basket with wide, 1 1/2" oak handle made by
Eugene Turner.

Copyright © 1987 by Jean Turner Finley.
Library of Congress Catalog Number: 86-60001.

All rights reserved. No part of this work may be reproduced or used in
any forms or by any means—graphic, electronic or mechanical,
including photocopying or information storage and retrieval systems—
without written permission from the copyright holder.

Printed in the United States of America.
ISBN: 0-88740-087-6
Published by Schiffer Publishing Ltd.
1469 Morstein Road, West Chester, Pennsylvania 19380

This book may be purchased from the publisher.
Please include $2.00 postage.
Try your bookstore first.

Contents

Two round hoops were used to make this basket's frame—one 14" and one 16", and the smaller handle hoop forced the larger one into an oval shape for the rim. 30 closely placed ribs make this a sturdy basket that is used for picnics by the owner. Made by Andrea Neighbors.

Christmas goose made by Claudia Young in grapevine nest. 10" Key basket made by Carolynn Schneider.

12" Scottish Yarn Basket. Made by Kirsten Gotzsche.

12" Scottish Yarn Basket. Bright goldenrod flat weavers and dark blue round ones were overdyed with natural walnut stain. Made by Kirsten Goetzsche.

Oval basket: round hoop with oval handle, approximately 10" x 15", 3/8" flat weavers. Finished with a gusset worked from the center toward the rim. Made by Anne Leighton.

8" x 12" rectangular basket: Pokeberry dyed round reed accent with walnut stained 1/4" flat. Made by Kirsten Gotzsche.

Preface

I began writing instructions at the request of those in my classes who wanted to make further baskets on their own. The construction of a basket can bring more than tangible rewards, and I enjoy seeing others experience these along with the satisfaction and joy of workmanship that making a basket brings.

Basketry has brought many bonuses to me that I had not anticipated. A group of us meets regularly to make baskets. We share ideas and learn from one another—usually managing to cover a variety of other topics as well. It's a fun time, and getting together to work with a congenial friend or group is something I highly recommend. Membership in our state basket makers' guild has been rewarding, and several chance meetings including "basket talk" with enthusiastic and friendly people in different parts of our country has made me increasingly aware of the wide scope of the craft. Basket makers seem to share a common language no matter where they live. I have come to realize that basketry and its traditions are a part of our heritage and it is to our advantage that they be preserved.

Introduction

Rib baskets have been made for centuries to meet specific agricultural and household needs. They were particularly common in the Appalachian mountains region of the United States, which includes the hilly portions of the Southern states of Tennessee, West Virginia, Kentucky, Virginia and North Carolina. The descriptive names, varying shapes, and uses of rib baskets relate information about the inventive people who made the baskets. From natural materials around them, these skilled craftspeople created an art form that continues to be appreciated.

Today, we can conserve our natural resources and still use traditional skills to weave our own authentically constructed baskets. We can purchase various kinds of commercial reed and make replicas of the original, or create useful and purely decorative baskets to fit our current lifestyles. These baskets will be our legacy for the future.

It is rewarding and creative to experiment with different kinds of basketry materials, and the weaving instructions given here may be applied to a large variety of them. If you are a beginner, first follow the directions as they are given. Soon you will find that you are comfortable with the craft and can adapt the instructions to make baskets of your own design.

Basic Tools

awl	masking tape
scissors	wood glue
knife	twist ties or clothes pins
measuring tape	twine or waxed thread
pencil sharpener to point the ribs	pan to soak the reed

*A battery powered pencil sharpener is a real time-saver.
**A glue gun is not included in the basic list but is frequently used by many basketmakers.

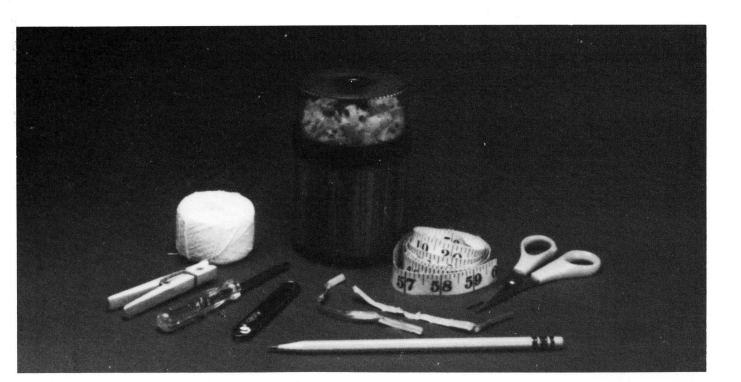

Basketry Materials

The commercial materials that are suggested in this book may be purchased at craft shops or businesses that specialize in chair caning. If shops in your area do not stock basketry supplies, there are many businesses throughout the United States that will fill orders by telephone or mail.

Natural materials vary widely, so do not expect all lengths of reed to be the same quality. No two baskets can ever be exactly alike; their variety adds to the beauty of handmade baskets.

Carnival hoops. Courtesy, The Canery, Winston-Salem, N.C.

Dogwood handles. Courtesy, The Canery, Winston-Salem, N.C.

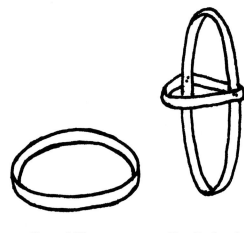

Round Hoop   Key Basket frame

Handle and rim hoops are sold by size. There is a great range of sizes, widths and shapes of the hoops used for handles and rims. Common widths of commercial hoops ("carnival hoops") range from 7/16" to 1". Carnival hoops are usually made from poplar or oak. Frames (2 or more hoops put together) can be purchased pre-assembled for some baskets.

One pound bundles of reed coiled. Courtesy, The Canery, Winston-Salem, N.C.

One pound bundles ("hanks") of reed. Courtesy, The Canery, Winston-Salem, N.C.

Round reed

a. Flat oval reed   b. Half round reed

Round reed is measured in millimeters, and progresses in size from #0, which is 1.5mm in diameter, to #10, which is 7mm in diameter. The smaller sizes (0 through 4) are pliable and can be used as weavers. The large sizes make good ribs and also can be fashioned into hoops and handles. Most sizes of round reed are bound into one pound coils and are sold by the pound.

Flat reed

Flat reed is available in eight widths: 3/16", 1/4", 3/8", 1/2", 5/8", 3/4", 7/8", and 1".

Larger sizes of both the flat and round reeds can be found, but they are not readily available. Flat reed may be purchased in one pound coils or hanks. It saves time in the long run if a newly purchased hank of reed is divided into short, medium and long lengths and each piece of reed is coiled and fastened with a twist tie until it is needed.

Flat oval reed has a flat underside with a smoothly curved top.
Half round reed has a flat underside with a half circular top. Both are sold by the width like flat reed.

Most of the baskets shown with the directions in this book can be constructed with three basic materials: carnival hoops, #6 round reed, and 1/4" flat reed.

Much of the commercial material used in basket making is called "reed", no matter what its origin is, even though reed is technically defined as "tall grass with a jointed, hollow stalk". Some commercial reed actually comes from bamboo, which is a grass; however, most commercial "reed" has been split from the inner core of rattan, a type of climbing palm. The rattan vine grows in tropical climates, and while its diameter may be only a few inches, it can be hundreds of feet in length. The shiny outside of rattan is split into strips called cane, which is used for chair caning, but can also be woven into baskets.

Sea grass ("Hong Kong" grass), **rush, paper cord,** and **raffia** are some of the other natural materials available. Different natural and synthetic materials can inspire ideas for different basket designs and uses.

9

Components

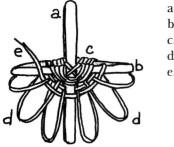

a. handle hoop
b. rim hoop
c. ears
d. ribs
e. weaver

a. through e.   parts of a basket.

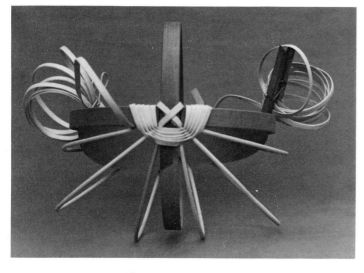

Hoops

Two round carnival hoops are put together to make the frame for a basic, curved rib basket.

1. The top part of the vertical hoop will be the basket's handle and its lower part, the center rib. The horizontal hoop will be the basket's rim.
2. Most of the commercially available hoops are formed by gluing together the ends of a flexible strip of wood. Since water will dissolve the glue, the spliced "joint" must be kept dry.
3. When the two hoops are put together, the rim hoop is usually placed inside and at right angles to the handle hoop. The joint of the handle hoop may be placed either at the base of the basket or at the rim, and the joint of the rim may be placed either at the handle hoop or on the side of the basket.
4. Your signature is an important part of every basket you weave. It may be written on a hoop with a wood burning tool or an indelible pen. Include the date along with your name or initials.

Ears

The two hoops are held together by reed which is woven or lashed around them. This reed may be bound simply around the hoops or woven in a design which is called an ear.

1. Most ears are woven with flat reed, which has both a smooth and a rough side. The smooth side of the reed is kept to the outside when the ears are made. Run the reed between your fingers to feel which is the rougher side.
2. Sometimes it is difficult to tell which side is which. Bend the reed and hold it to the light. The rough side will show small breaks or splinters.

Ribs

Ribs are inserted in the ears and outline the shape that the basket will have when it is finished. The lengths of the ribs which are given in the instructions that follow were used in the baskets shown as examples. If you are a novice basket maker, follow the directions as they are given. The result will be a basket that is very similar to the example, but because basketry materials are never exactly the same, yours will still be a unique creation.

1. After the ends of the ribs have been inserted in the ears and a few rows woven across them, check the outline they make to see if it conforms to the final shape you have in mind. Hold the basket facing an ear. Imagine a line drawn from rim to rim, touching the outer-most curve of each rib. This is how the basket will look when the spaces between the ribs have been filled with weaving. If this shape is not satisfactory, the rib lengths may be adjusted.

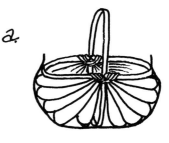

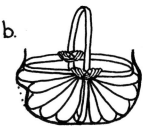

Outline made by ribs

The ribs in diagram *a* need no adjustment. Rib #2 in diagram *b* is much too short, and a new rib must be cut to replace it. The example has been exaggerated for the purpose of illustration. There is rarely so much difference, but some adjustment is often required.

2. Before removing the ends of a rib from an ear or the weaving, slide an awl alongside it to hold the weaving in place until the rib is ready to be re-inserted, then slide the rib back in beside the awl before removing the awl. If a rib is too long, pull only one end from the weaving and cut it shorter. A rib that is only slightly too short or too long can be adjusted by pulling it outward a trifle, or by inserting it a bit further into the weaving or ear.

3. Use the suggested measurements as guides, but use your eye to make the final decision. After only a little experience, it will be easier and faster to hold a length of reed in the place it is to be inserted and to cut the rib by sight. Sharpen one end of the reed with a pencil sharpener or a knife and insert the sharpened end in the ear or the weaving. Curve the reed so that it follows the outline planned for the basket. Lay the rest of the reed on top of the ear or the weaving on the other side of the basket, and cut it at the point where that end is to be inserted.

4. Taper or shave the ends of the ribs with a pencil sharpener or a knife for smooth insertion and concealment in the weavers. The ends of the first, "primary", ribs that are used are inserted in the ears.

5. The space between two ribs will be narrow at the ears and become wider toward the middle of the basket. As the weaving progresses, the space between two ribs may become too wide to offer enough support for the weaving reed. Further "secondary" ribs may be added between them to tighten the weaving. Thread the ends of a secondary rib through the weaving alongside a primary rib, and conceal them behind a row of weaving. Check the outline of the basket when secondary ribs are added and adjust the rib lengths if necessary. Generally, secondary ribs in baskets made with #6 round reed ribs and ¼" flat reed weavers are added when the distance between two ribs is about 1½". However, this is a matter of personal preference and depends on the final appearance one wants to achieve. For instance, loosely woven reed will result in a more primitive appearance than tightly woven reed.

6. Secondary ribs are always added in pairs. When a secondary rib is added to one side of the basket, a corresponding rib must be added to the other side. After new ribs have been added, the weaving pattern will be out of phase in the next row, but the weave will correct itself in the following row.

7. Heavier reed does not often curve uniformly and will need to be re-shaped before it can be used for ribs. To shape the reed, cut it into lengths a little longer than the ribs will be. Soak the lengths in water. Curve the lengths along the outside of a hoop and fasten them to the hoop with twist ties or clips. Allow the reed to dry thoroughly (at least 24 hours) before removing.

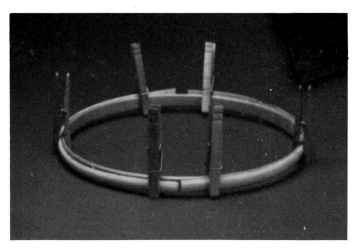

Flat oval reed is shaped around a carnival hoop.

Weavers

Long strips of flexible reed used to make the ears and to weave the body of the basket are called **weavers**.

1. Before a weaver is used, it must be dampened. Soak the weaving reed in water until it is pliable. There is a considerable difference in the time that different reeds must be soaked before they are ready for use. Less than a minute is often sufficient for thin reeds while 20 minutes or more will be required for some of the thicker ones. Wrap the wet weaver around your finger. If it bends easily, it is ready to use. Reed that is too dry will crack and break; reed that is too wet will split apart and shred. **Never** weave with dry reed. A plastic spray bottle or the spray attachment on a kitchen sink is helpful for re-wetting weavers that have begun to dry.

2. For purposes of illustration, most of the weaving in the diagrams in this book is shown beginning from the left of the handle. Whether you prefer to start from the right or from the left, it is important to be consistent. Always begin to weave from the same side of the handle, bringing the weaver over or under the same ribs in both halves of the basket.

3. Near the ears, the spaces between the ribs are sometimes very small, and the weaving will be smoother if the weaver is trimmed to a narrower width for the first few rows. Start from the rim and trim the outside edge of the weaver until a workable width is reached, gradually broadening back again to the original width —OR— taper the reed sharply inside the rim as shown.

4. Keep the weaver taut while working, but be careful. If pulled too tight, the ribs and rim will be bent out of shape. If one weaver pulls the rim downward, a gap will be left between the top of the rim and the weavers in other rows. Instead of pulling the weaver around the rim, smooth it snugly against the sides and top with your thumb.

5. Push each new row of weaving against the previous one, keeping in mind that wet reed shrinks crosswise against the grain, so it will not be quite as wide after it has dried.

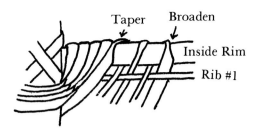

Beginning weaver was tapered to a narrow width for the first few rows but has now been slanted back to its original 1/4''.

From left: 6'' oval Roll Basket. 3'' Egg Basket. 12'' Hen Basket with #2 smoked round reed weavers. 5'' x 9'' oval Egg Basket with oil base ''Black Walnut'' stain made by Marian Ward.

General Directions for all Rib Baskets

These general instructions apply to all of the particular basket styles covered in this book and should be read and understood before you begin to make your basket. They will be referred to as you proceed through the particular project you choose.

For the exact materials and quantities needed for your project, see the section on your chosen basket style as presented in this book. Then relate the instructions given there to these general instructions and you will be able to create your own basket.

Materials: (see specific project in this book for amounts and sizes.)

    Carnival hoops (rim and handle)
    Round reed (ribs)
    Flat reed (weavers)

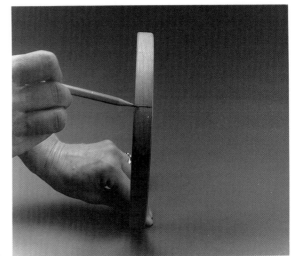

Step 1.

General Construction Techniques

Step 1.

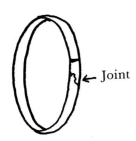

← Joint

1. Choose one hoop for the basket's handle. Find where its ends have been joined and glued together. Draw a light line across the outside of the hoop 1½ to 2 inches above this joint.

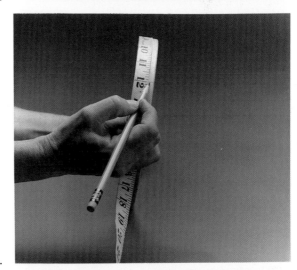

Step 2.

Step 2.
Mark handle length

measure

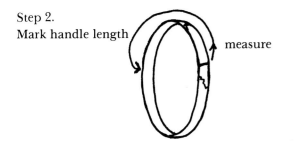

2. Measure the desired handle length from the straight line over the top of the hoop. Mark the handle length by drawing another line on the other side of the hoop. Lightly pencil an X on the hoop about halfway between these two lines to show the top of the basket.

Step 2.

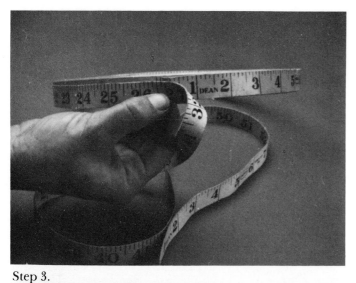

Step 3.

Step 3.

Step 4a.

Step 3.

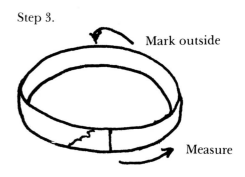

Mark outside

Measure

3. Measure the circumference of the rim hoop, and divide by two. Draw a straight line lightly across the outside of the hoop 1½ to 2 inches from its joint. Measure half the circumference from this line and mark with another line across the hoop.

Step 4.

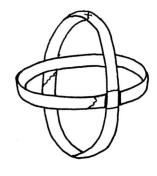

a.

b.

c.

d.

4. Put the hoops together:

a. Hold the rim hoop with its joint side toward you and to the **left** of the rim line. Hold the handle hoop with the X on top and its joint on the side that is away from you. Slide the handle hoop over the rim with the X on top, and the handle and rim joints on opposite sides.

b. Hold the hoops with the rim joint toward you and to the left of the rim line. Place the top edge of the rim just below the line on the handle hoop. Place the handle hoop just to the left of the rim line.

c. Two more lines may be drawn to outline where the hoops meet—one across the handle hoop just below the rim, and one on the rim along the left side of the handle hoop.

d. Rotate the hoops halfway so that the joint of the handle hoop is toward you. Keep the X on top. **Do not turn the hoops upside down when you rotate them.** Position as on the other side with the top edge of the rim just below the line on the handle hoop, and the handle hoop just to the left of the rim line. Two more lines may be drawn to outline where the hoops meet.

5. Check the measurements. The two exposed portions of the rim should be the same length. Reposition the rim, if necessary, keeping the rim joint to the left of the handle.

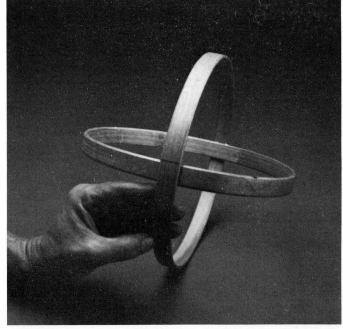

Step 4b.

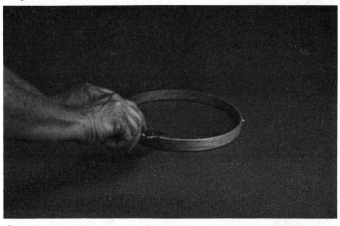

Step 6a. Notches are cut for twine.

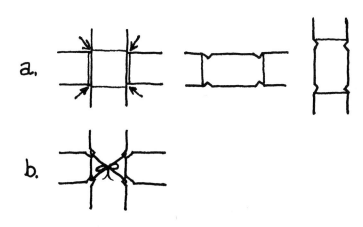

6. Tie, or glue the hoops together. -OR— Cut notches in them to hold twine, then tie them for a firm hold:

a. Cut 4 small notches on each side of the rim and on each side of the handle hoop with a knife.

b. Put the hoops back together at the notches and tie to hold. (Wet the twine first, and it will be easier to tie.)

7. Soak a length of the flat weaving reed in water until it is pliable (pg. 11, Weavers #1).

8. Weave the ears with flat reed—smooth side out. Before beginning, check the X to make sure handle portion is on top.

Step 6b.

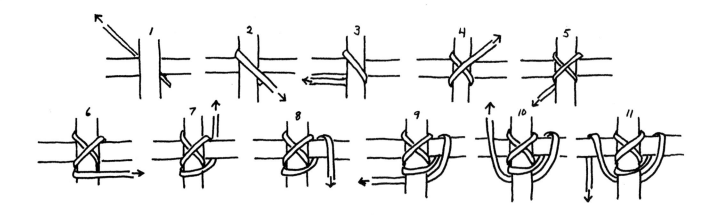

Ear or Three-fold Lashing

The first 5 steps are only worked once. After step #11, go back to step #6 and work steps #6 through #11 about four more times for a medium size basket. Overlap the edges of the weavers slightly, but keep the ear as flat as possible. End at the left of the handle as in step #11.

Do not cut the remaining reed as it will be used to start to weave the ribs. Keep it clipped to the rim or handle until you have inserted the ribs in the ear and are ready to begin weaving.

Ear Step 1.

Ear Step 2.

Ear Step 3. The Weaver is brought around and over the beginning end.

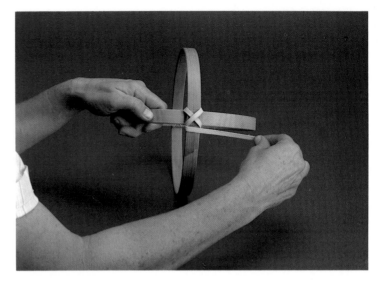

Ear Step 6.

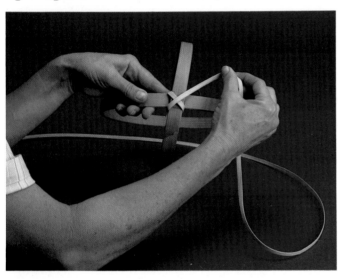

Ear Step 4.

Ear Step 7. & 8.

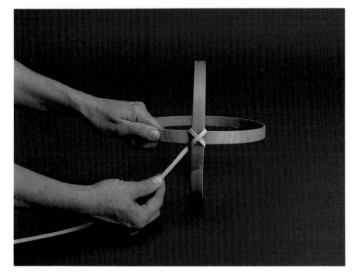

Ear Step 5.

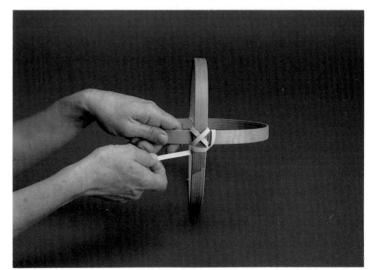

Ear Step 9.

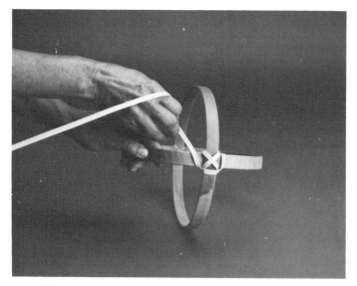

Ear Step 10.

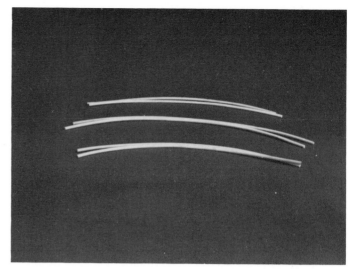

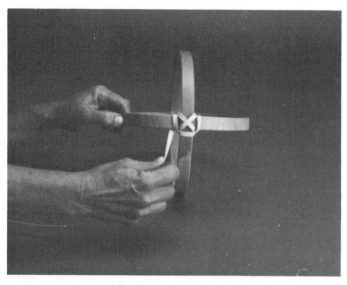

Ear Step 11. Repeat steps #6 through #11, overlapping weaver edges slightly until ear is the size desired (about 4 more times for a medium size basket.)

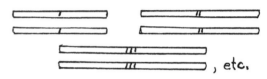

9. Cut primary ribs by sight or by the measurements suggested in the directions for making your specific basket. When the ribs are of different lengths, identify them by penciling the same number in the middle of each of the two ribs in a pair.

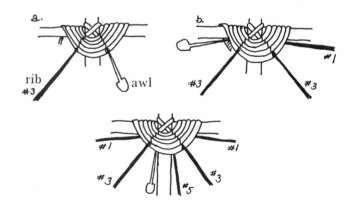

10. Sharpen the ends of the ribs with a pencil sharpener or a knife, and place rib pairs #3, #1 and #5: Remoisten the ears.

a. With an awl, pierce one side of an ear at its mid-point (where the reed crosses.) With a slight twist, insert the pointed end of a #3 rib in the hole. Pierce a corresponding hole in the opposite ear, and insert the other end of the rib there. Repeat with the second #3 rib in the other halves of the ears.

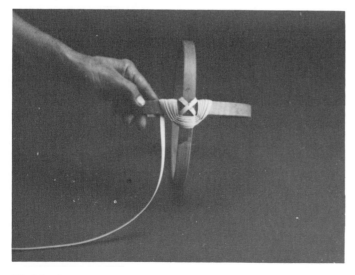

Finished ear.

18

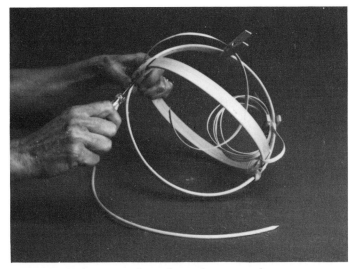

Step 10a. Using an awl to pierce the ear reed.

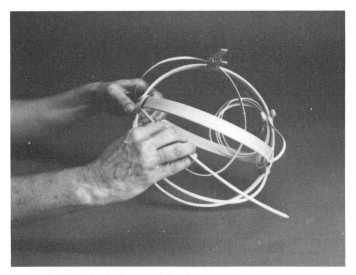

Step 10b. Rib #1 is inserted in the ear.

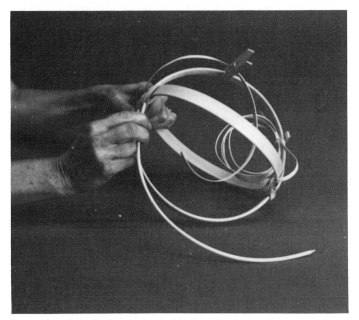

Step 10a. Rib #3 is inserted.

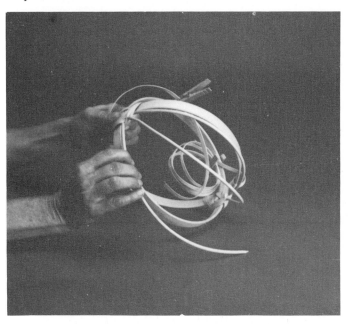

Step 10b. Rib #5 is inserted.

b. Insert the ends of the #1 ribs into the small open spaces in the ears just below the rim. The ribs should not fall directly below the rim but should curve slightly beyond it. Insert the #5 ribs on either side of the handle base. The awl helps to separate the reed and enlarge the openings, but the ears are pierced only at their mid-points.

The first rows of weaving will be worked over these six primary ribs, the lower part of the handle hoop (now the center rib), and the rim.

11. The ribs outline the basic shape of the finished basket. Before proceeding, check the outline they make to see if it conforms to the shape you want, and make any necessary adjustments in the lengths of the ribs before proceeding. (pg. 10, Ribs #1).

Step 11. Primary ribs inserted.

Step 12.

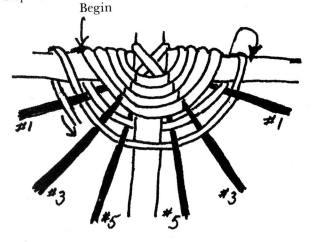

After only a little experience, it is easier and faster to hold a long length of reed in place and to cut the rib by sight. Start with the first rib below the rim. Sharpen one end and insert it in the ear. Curve the reed so that it extends slightly beyond the rim and lies against the other ear. Cut the reed to size; sharpen the second end and insert it in the other ear. Repeat in the other half of the basket so that both halves will be the same. Follow the same procedure with the rest of the ribs.

12. Dampen the reed remaining from one of the ears. Starting at the left of the handle, bring reed ("weaver") under the rim, over rib #1, under #3, over #5, under the handle base (now the center rib), over #5, etc. to the rim on the other side. Bring the reed around the rim and weave back across to the rim at the left of the handle. Repeat. You will have woven four rows. *Note: The weaver may be trimmed to a narrower width for the first few rows (pg. 12, #3.)*

Note: Weave only one or two ribs at a time. Grasp the weaver a few inches from where it leaves the basket, and slide it sideways through the space between two ribs. This will lessen the chance of the ribs being pushed out of shape by a weaver that is pulled too tight. Instead of pulling the weaver around the rim, smooth it firmly against the side of the rim with your thumb.

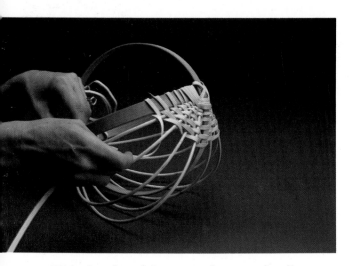

Step 12. One row has been woven across the ribs.

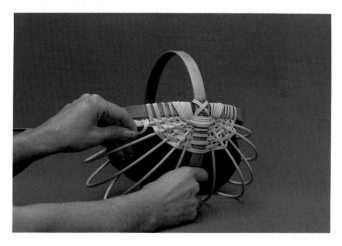

Correct technique.

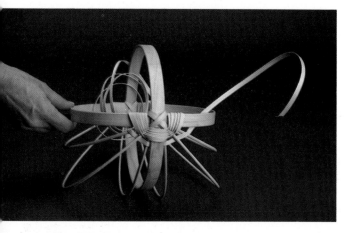

Slide the edge of the weaver between the ribs.

Note: The lengths of a basket's ribs determine the shapes of its sides. Baskets of the same style may have sides which range in shape from flat to fully rounded. In the specific directions for the baskets that follow, the suggested rib lengths may be followed exactly and will result in a basket that is very similar to the one that is shown. However, since natural materials are not all alike, don't be surprised if the two are not exactly the same. Use the suggested measurements as guides, but use your eye to make the final decision.

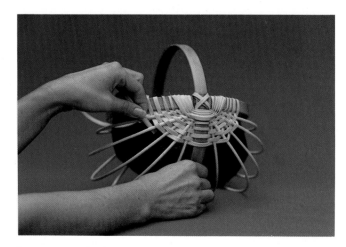

Incorrect technique.

20

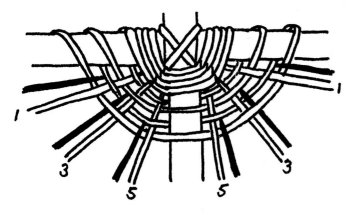

Secondary ribs.

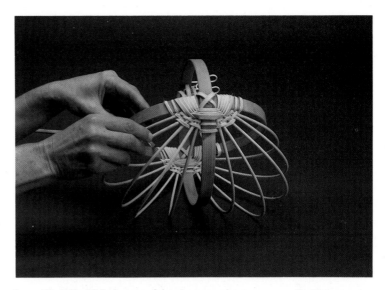

Step 13. Rib #2 is inserted in the weaving next to rib #3.

13. Add the secondary ribs. They may be placed on either side of the primary ones—whichever fills the spaces better—but they should be added in the same way to each half of the basket. When ribs are added to one half, an equal number must be added to the other. Always insert both ends of a secondary rib against the same primary rib. Conceal the sharpened ends behind the weaving. Weave just enough to hold the ribs in place. Check the outline that they form, and make any necessary adjustments in their lengths. Further weaving will hold them firmly and make it difficult to do so later. If a rib must be pulled from the weaving to shorten or replace it, insert an awl through the weaving beside it before removing the rib. The awl will take its place until you are ready to re-insert the rib. Remember that after new ribs have been added, the weaving pattern in the next row will be irregular but will correct itself in the following row.

14. Weave the remainder of the basket, adding more ribs to help shape it or to keep the weaving from becoming loose when the spaces widen between the ribs (pg. 11, #5). When weaving over #6 round ribs with ¼" weavers, additional ribs are usually added when the width between two ribs is 1½ to 2 inches. This is a matter of personal taste and depends on how firmly woven the weaver wants the basket to be.

15. After you come to the end of a weaver, move to the other side of the basket to begin a new one. Alternately weaving one side and then the other will help maintain the basket's shape.

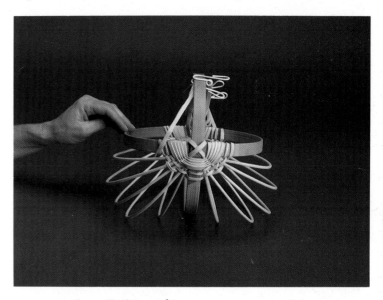

Two secondary ribs inserted.

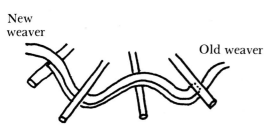

New weaver

Old weaver

16. To add a new weaver, place the beginning end of the new weaver over a few inches of the one that is ending. Conceal the cut end of the new weaver beneath a rib. Weave the overlapping reeds together until the new weaver is secure. Conceal the end of the "old" weaver between the new weaver and a rib.

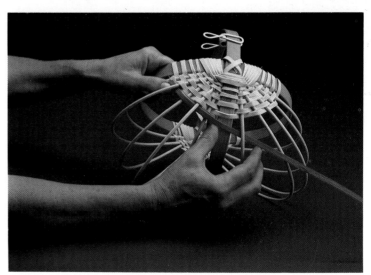

Step 16. The new red weaver is added by overlapping it with the other and weaving the two together—across 4 ribs in this instance.

21

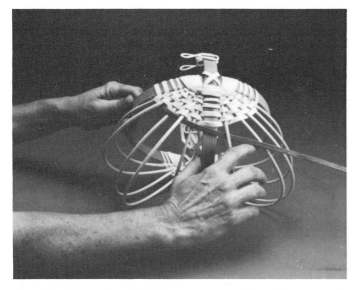

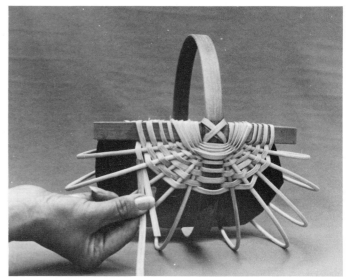

Step 16. The ends of both weavers are placed between the other weaver and a rib.

Step 16. Adding a new weaver.

17. When the entire basket has been woven, the weavers from each side will meet. Finish by concealing the ends and overlapping as illustrated by diagram on preceeding page.

Note: It is better to add new weavers and new ribs at different times. Add a new weaver earlier than necessary to keep from having to do so at a critical place.

18. In larger baskets, especially those in which the ribs vary considerably in length, it is often a good idea to stop weaving from the ears after all the ribs have been added. Start a new weaver in the middle of the basket and weave several rows toward each ear. These rows will help keep the ribs from being pushed out of shape as the weaving then continues from the ears. Fold a new weaver over the middle of the rim. Clip to hold it in place. Starting with one half of the weaver, weave several rows toward one ear; then with the other half, weave the same number of rows toward the opposite ear. Add new weavers by overlapping as usual, alternating the weaving first toward one ear, then toward the other.

Note: The weaving pattern of the middle weavers must be the same as that of the ear weavers coming toward them so their ends can be overlapped when they meet. i.e. Weavers traveling across the ribs in opposite directions must cover the same ribs. Weavers traveling across the ribs in the same direction must cover alternate ribs.

Step 18.

Fold

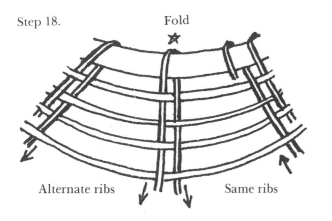

Alternate ribs   Same ribs

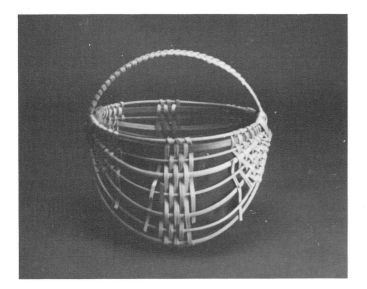

Arrows on short strips of reed show the directions of the weavers in the rows beside them.

Finishing

1. The twine at the ears may be clipped and pulled out any time after the ears are made.

2. Erase any visible pencil marks.

3. Small gaps in the finished weaving may be filled after the basket has been dampened by covering them with short pieces of reed anchored in the weaving (pg. 37, Note). This may also be done while the basket is being woven. Cut a small piece from the end of the weaver you are using and insert it behind ribs on either side of the opening.

4. Most baskets will retain their form without further shaping, but one of the following procedures may be used:

a. Cut two scrap pieces of wood to size. Moisten the basket (excepting joints) and wedge one wood piece between the insides of the rim and one between the top of the handle and its base. Let the basket dry completely before removing the wedges; the basket will retain its shape.

b. Tie string from one hoop to another. The tension from the string will often pull the weavers into a more satisfactory shape.

c. Place a heavy weight in the bottom of the basket. This will help to flatten one that tends to roll or tip to one side.

Note: Do not try to make a radical change in shape. Too much pressure can pull the hoops apart and damage or break them and the reeds.

Make sure that air can circulate around a damp basket and prevent mold from forming while the basket dries.

5. Small splinters can be removed by cutting them off with scissors, by smoothing them with fine sandpaper or an emery board or by rotating the basket over an open flame. If they are to be burned off, dampen the entire basket and let it rest until just the splinters are dry before beginning to sear them. The flame must be quickly extinguished to prevent scorching the rest of the basket.

6. The natural materials of the basket will darken in color over a period of time, but they may also be stained with either chemical or natural dyes. Unless otherwise noted, a stain made simply by soaking black walnuts in water was used for most of the baskets in the illustrations.

Antique baskets were rarely stained as the purpose for making them was to fill a need, and the sooner the basket was ready to be used, the better. Many of these older baskets have aged to a beautiful patina.

7. After a time, a naturally stained or untreated basket tends to dry and become brittle; but with a little care, it will retain its beauty and resiliency for many years. It is important to dampen a basket at least once a year, or more often if it has been kept in a very dry place. Spray the basket or dip it in water to add the needed moisture. A very fragile basket can be left near a bathroom shower where it will be gradually moistened by the high humdity.

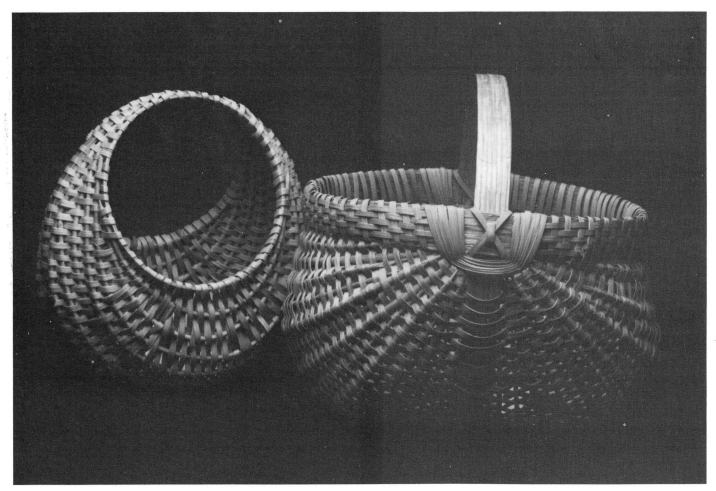

Decorative Options

Woven Handle

After the hoops have been put together, cut two lengths of round reed long enough to lay against the edges of the handle, with their ends extending just below the rim. Shave the ends flat, and secure the reeds to the handle with masking tape. The ends of both the reeds and the weaver will be hidden and held in place by the ears. Begin to weave by bringing the weaver, smooth side out, up from behind the rim to the left of the handle. Pull it between the round reed and the handle, over the reed, etc., as shown. Keep the round reeds even with the handle's edges as you weave.

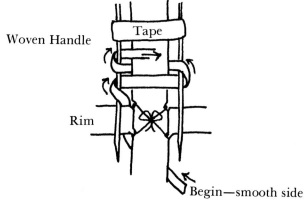

Woven Handle

Tape

Rim

Begin—smooth side of reed out

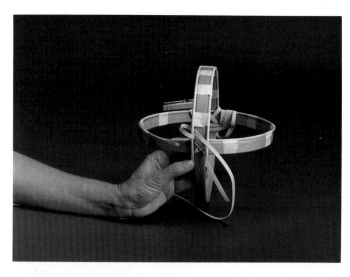

Beginning to weave the handle.

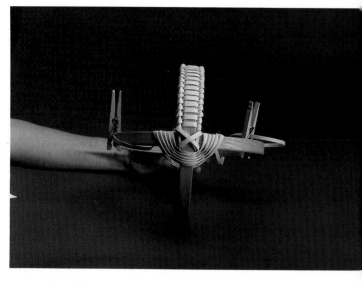

Woven handle.

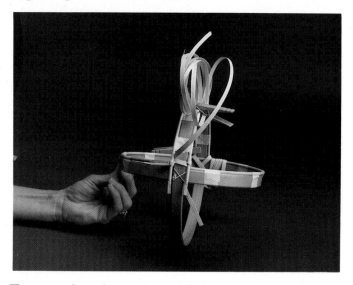

Two rows have been woven. The second row is across the back of the handle.

Woven Rim

1. Lay a single piece of round reed around the top edge of the rim. Overlap the ends of the reed about a half inch near the handle. Shave the insides of the overlapping ends halfway through the reed so when they are put together, their diameter will be the same as the uncut reed. Tape the round reed to the top edge of the rim with masking tape. When the basket is woven, the edging reed may be lifted upward slightly to make room for a weaver to pass between it and the rim. However, if pulled too firmly near the ear, the overlapping ends may become so far apart that the ear reed will be left with no support.

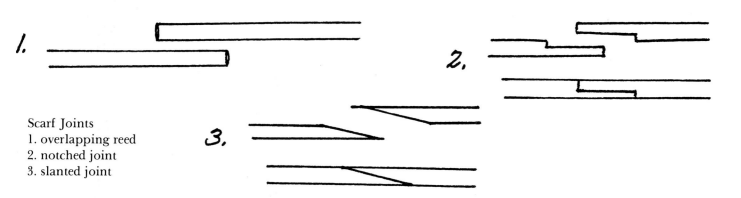

Scarf Joints
1. overlapping reed
2. notched joint
3. slanted joint

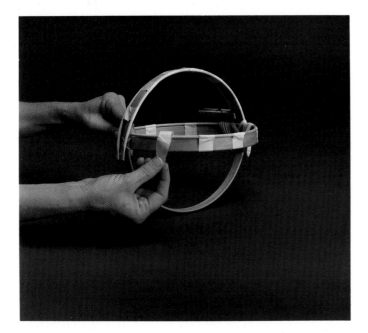

Round reed is taped to the edge of the rim.

2. Cut two pieces of round reed and lay them on top of the rim with their ends tapered and just touching the sides of the handle. Secure them to the rim with masking tape. The gradual tapering of the ends allows them to be pulled a short way from the handle when the rim is woven, still leaving enough support for the ears.

Woven Rim

1. Scarf ends   Shave inside

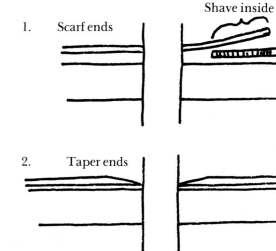

2. Taper ends

Woven Rim

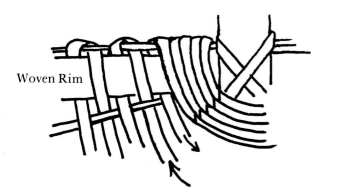

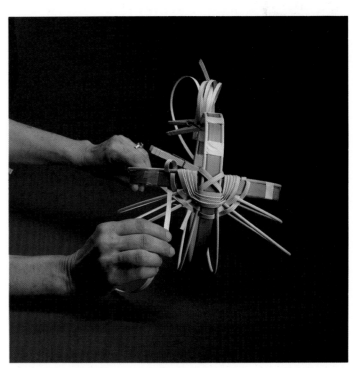

Weaving the rim...(This handle will be woven after the basket is, however it is easier to do so before any weaving is added to the rest of the frame.)

Bowknot or Three-fold Variation

Steps 1 through 10—"Bowknot Ear".

Bowknot, step 1.

Bowknot, step 4.

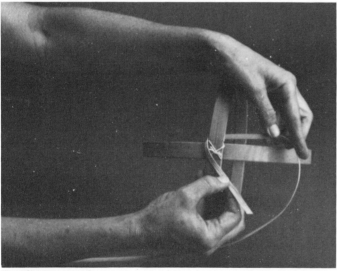

Bowknot, step 2.

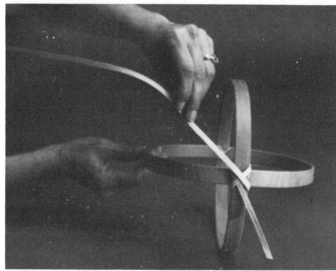

Bowknot, step 5.

Bowknot, step 3.

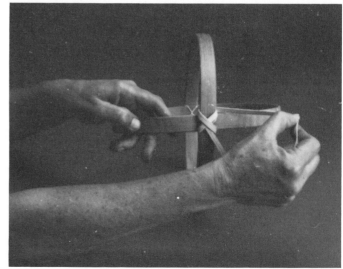

Bowknot, step 6.

Bowknot, step 7.

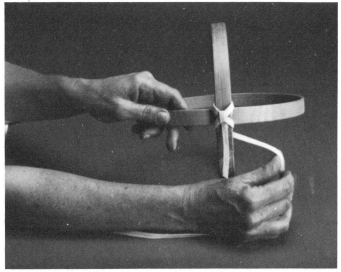

Bowknot, step 10

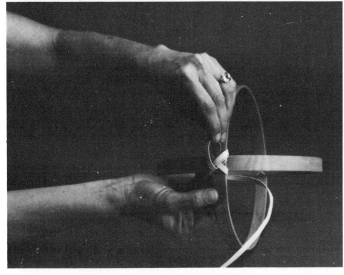

Bowknot, step 8.

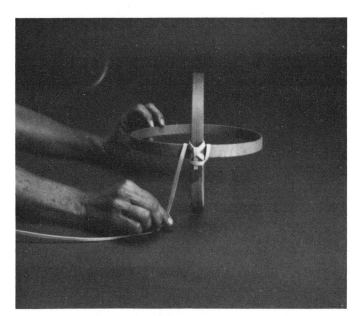

Finish the same as for a plain 3-fold ear.

Bowknot, step 9.

Step #9: The beginning end of the weaver is looped up and inserted behind the "X" made by the intersection of the reed, then it is pulled down between the reed and the hoop. An awl will help make an opening for the weaver. Cutting the end of the weaver so that it slants to a point is also helpful if the space is tight.

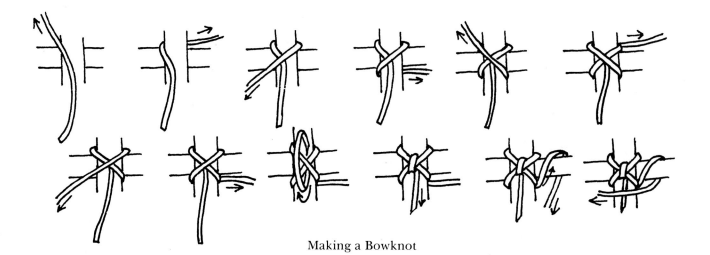

Making a Bowknot

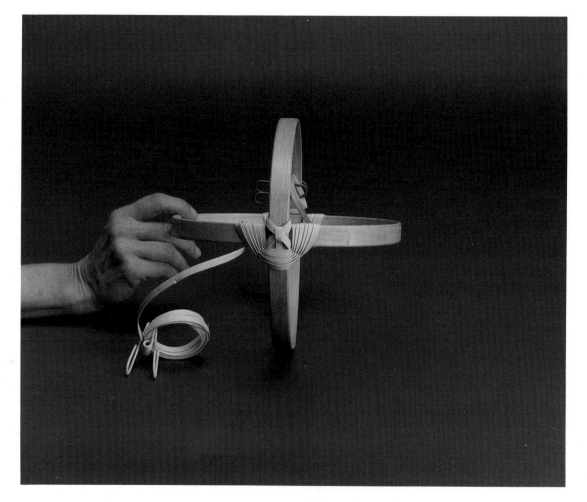

Finished Bowknot.

God's eye, step 1.

God's eye, step 4.

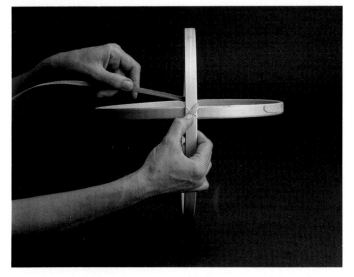

God's eye, step 2.

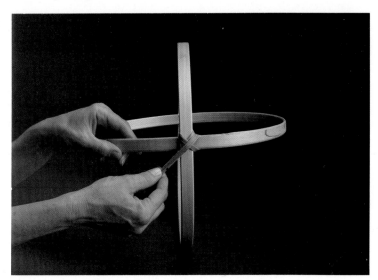

God's eye, step 5.

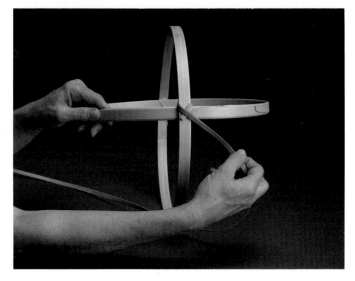

God's eye, step 3.

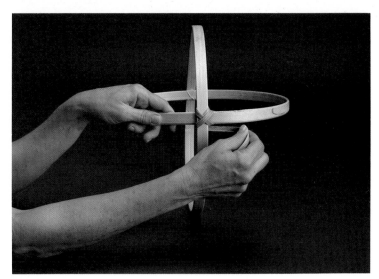

God's eye, step 6.

God's eye, step 7.

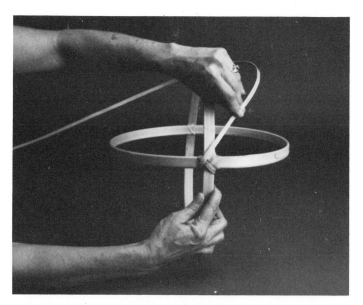

God's eye, step 9.

God's eye, step 8.

God's eye, step 10.

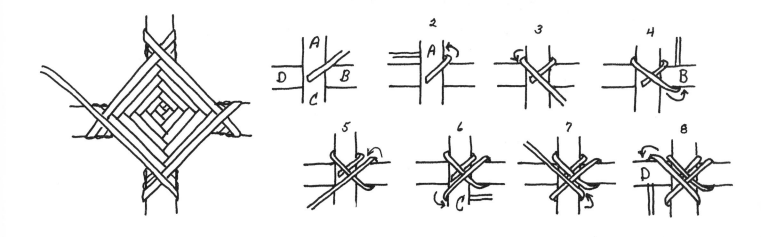

The god's eye ear is most effective on medium and large size baskets. It creates a pocket that will hold the ribs in place, and it eliminates the use of an awl to pierce or separate the reed. Begin with roughly an eight foot length of pliable reed. Overlap the edges of the weaver just slightly and keep the ear as flat as possible. Repeat the pattern below until the ear is the size desired, ending with the weaver behind the rim as in step #8. It is often a good idea to trim the reed to about half its width for the first few rows of weaving (pg. 12 #3).

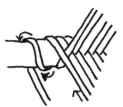

Wrapped once around rim, *Note (b).*

Alternate finish for god's eye, *Note (a).*

Alternate finish for god's eye.

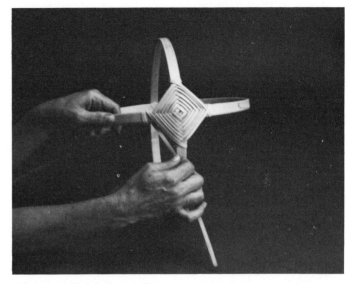

Alternate finish for god's eye.

Note: The final diagonal weaver may be tightened by bringing it under the outermost weaver on the rim (a.). The first weaver may cross the rim so close to the ear that it exerts pressure and tends to force the ear weavers back toward the handle, loosening the reed and pushing the ear out of shape. An alternative is to wrap the weaver once around the rim before beginning to weave the ribs (b.).

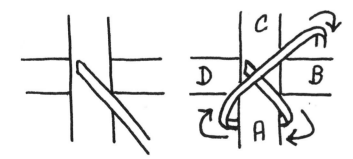

Optional beginning for changing to different reed.

One kind of reed may be used to weave the god's eye and another to weave the ribs. Begin the ear by placing the end of the reed on the handle hoop as shown. Bring the weaver diagonally down to the lower right corner, then straight behind the hoop to the left. Proceed in a counterclockwise direction with the god's eye pattern, ending in the middle of the basket instead of at the rim.

Inside ear

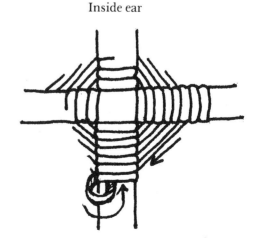

Optional finish

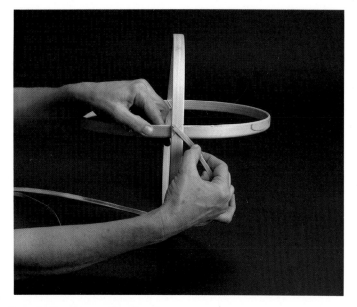

Step 1. Position of beginning weaver for a god's eye that will finish on the back of the center hoop.

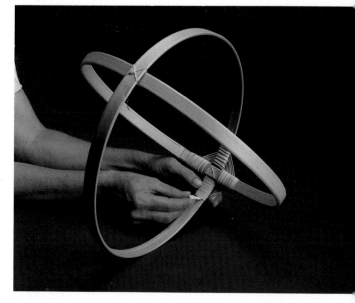

The weaver is placed under the center hoop wraps to finish the god's eye.

Step 2. Bring weaver straight across inside of center hoop.

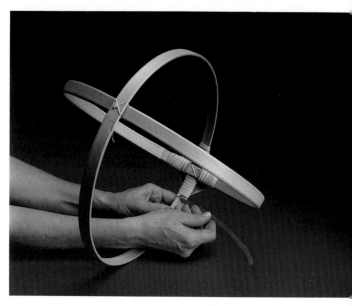

A different weaver is added.

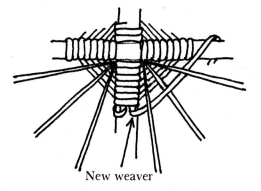

New weaver added to God's eye

Finish by tucking the end of the weaver under the lower wraps on the handle hoop. The awl will help lift the reed so the weaver can be inserted.

Anchor a new weaver at the same place, and begin weaving the ribs from the middle of the basket toward the rim.

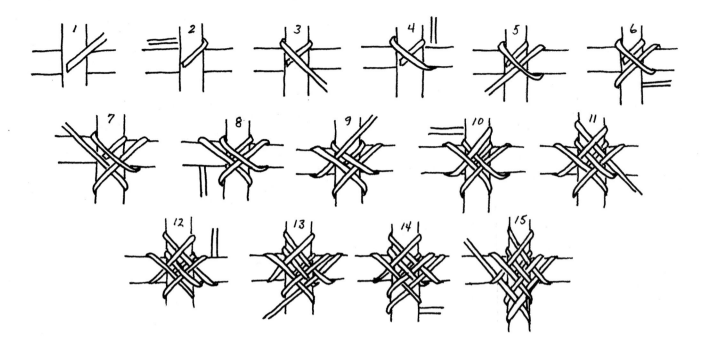

Braided God's Eye

The weaver edges do not overlap in a braided god's eye, but each row should be kept as close to the next as possible. When crossing diagonally, bring the weaver under each of the two outside rows, i.e. under itself, over the middle, and under the outermost row. The braided pattern starts at step #5 when the weaver comes from behind the rim and is brought under itself on the front. After step #10, the diagonal weaver will always go under both itself and the outermost weaver. Use the awl to lift the outermost weaver so you can pass beneath it. Slanting the end of the weaver is also helpful. When the ear reaches the desired size, insert the ribs and start weaving the basket from the left of the handle.

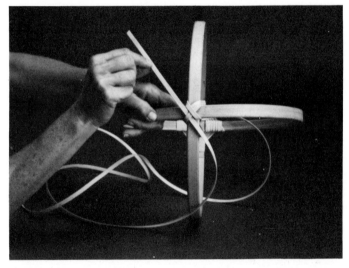

Step 7.

Step 5. The weaver crosses beneath the reed. It will be shifted to the left so that it crosses the hoops diagonally.

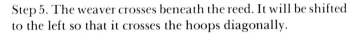

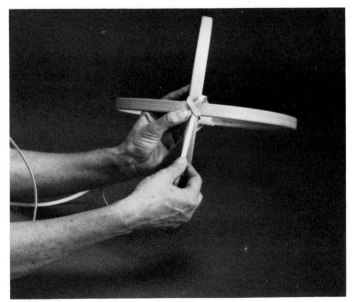

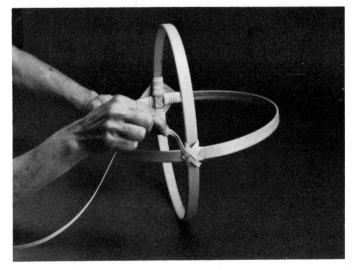

Step 8. The weaver crosses beneath the reed.

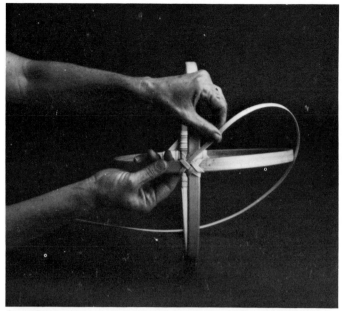

Step 9.

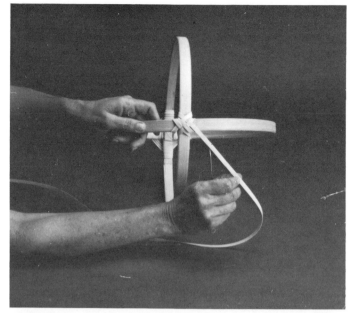

Step 12.

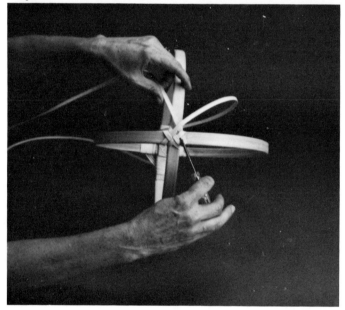

Step 11. The awl helps to open a space for the weaver to be inserted.

Braided god's eye, finished.

Compensation

When there is a considerable difference in the lengths of the ribs in a basket, several more rows of weaving are required to cover the longer ribs. As work on such a basket progresses, it becomes increasingly obvious that the shorter ribs and hoops will be completely filled with weaving before the longer ones are covered. A novice basket maker will find it takes only a little experience to help determine which of the methods for filling the longer ribs he or she prefers to use.

Note: The spaces between the rows of weavers are for the purpose of illustration. Each new row should be as close as possible to the one preceding it.

around it. When it is no longer possible to weave the rim, weave only to the first rib below it and reverse the weaver around that rib. Weave across to the other side of the basket, and reverse again around the first rib. Do not continue with this weaver, but pick up the weaver coming from the other half of the basket and weave only to the next rib below the first one. Reverse around it; weave across to the other side and reverse again around the second rib. Drop this weaver and go back to the first to weave the next row. Continue in this manner reversing around the ribs and alternating weavers after each row until the weaving has filled in. Conceal the ends of the reed in the weaving, or overlap them to finish.

Note: If the lower ribs and center hoop become filled with weaving before the middle ribs are covered, add new weavers and complete each side separately.

1b.

New weaver

b. Sometimes there is only enough space on the rim or a rib for one width of the weaving reed. Instead of looping the weaver to reverse direction, cut the reed and place its end inside the basket. Drop down to the next rib, and begin a new weaver to return. The ends of both weavers may be hidden between a woven row and a rib, or they may be left to show inside the basket, whatever works better.

2

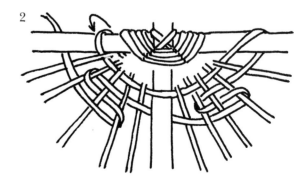

2. Basic Increasing

Extra weaving as close to the ears as possible will result in a smoother look in the finished weaving than if only a gusset is used. This is especially true when some ribs are considerably longer than others.

1a.

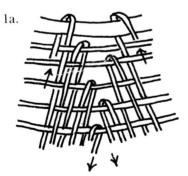

1. Gusset

a. Weave across the basket from rim to rim until the weavers from each half meet in the middle of the rim and are so close together there is not enough room to bring any more reed

The dark weaver shows increasing on middle ribs in each side of the basket.

The dark weaver shows the second row of increasing.

Weave from the rim until the longer ribs have been crossed. Reverse the weaver around the last long rib crossed, then weave back across only those long ribs which need extra weaving to fill them. Reverse again around a rib and continue to the other side. Do not weave to the rim. Weave only until the same long ribs have been crossed on this side, reversing around the one that is nearest the rim to weave them again before reversing and continuing to the rim.

When this is to be worked more than once, do not increase in adjoining rows but weave at least one row from rim to rim before increasing again. Increase most often on just the longest ribs.

If extra weaving is also needed to fill the rim or the center hoop, rows of increasing may be added to them in the same way they are added to the longer ribs.

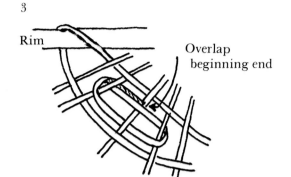

3

Rim

Overlap beginning end

Increasing.

3. **Filling-In**

Pause when the weaver reaches the longer ribs. Cut a separate strip of reed. Weave the long ribs back and forth, and overlap the ends to secure. Then continue with the original weaver. Although this may be done while a basket is being woven, it is most often used to fill loosely woven areas in a finished basket.

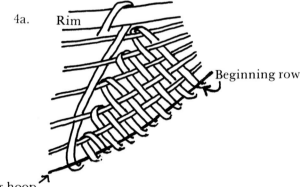

4a.   Rim

Beginning row

Center hoop

4. **Stepping Back** or **Stepping Up**

a. For baskets with the longer ribs near the base—Starting with the weaver in the last row woven from an ear, "side

Stepping back.

Stepping back.

"weaver", weave across the center hoop and up to the unfilled rib farthest from the hoop. Reverse around that rib; weave back across the hoop to the other side, and reverse around the same rib there. Continue in this way, reversing each time around the next ribs down, until extra rows on both sides have been added to all of the longer ribs and the center hoop. If necessary, an extra loop may also be added to the center hoop. (This procedure may be reversed. i.e. After crossing the center hoop, reverse the weaver first around the rib closest to it, then the next rib up, etc.)

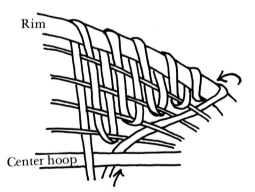

4b.

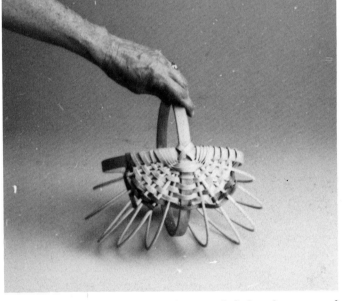

The short dark reed covers the gap left by the rows of increasing.

b. For baskets with the longer ribs near the rim—Bring the side weaver around the rim. Loop it back around the rim, then weave just the first rib below it. Reverse around that rib, and weave back around the rim. Weave only to the next rib below the first. Reverse around it and return to the rim. Continue in this manner, dropping down each time to reverse around the next rib, until extra rows have been added to all of the longer ribs and the rim on one side of the basket. Then weave across the center hoop and compensate in the same way on the other. (This procedure may also be reversed. i.e. Reverse the weaver first around the unfilled rib farthest from the rim, then the next rib up, etc.)

Note: Compensation often leaves small open spaces or gaps that may be covered by placing a short piece of the weaving reed over them. Overlap the ends of the reed with weavers on each side of the space, and conceal them beneath the ribs. The gaps are usually smaller when the compensation is closer to the ear than the middle of the basket.

Rib Baskets to Make:

Melon Basket

12" MELON BASKET

This is a good first basket for the novice to weave. All of the ribs may be cut from round reed instead of both flat oval and round as suggested below. If this is your first basket, use 10" instead of 12" hoops and #6 round reed for all of the ribs.

Materials:

    Two, 12" carnival hoops (handle and rim)
    ½" flat oval reed (6 primary ribs)
    #6 round reed (secondary ribs)
    ¼" flat reed (weavers)

Shape the flat oval reed around the hoops before starting construction (page 11, #7). Cut 6 lengths, each a little longer than the ribs are to be. These will be cut to the correct size when it is time to insert the ribs in the ears, (step #5 below). Soak the lengths in water until they are pliable. Lay them along the outsides of the two hoops, and attach them with twist ties or clips to the hoops. Wait until they are completely dry before removing—at least 24 hours.

Construction:

1. Measure, and mark both the handle and rim hoops the same as in step #3, pg. 14.
2. Lightly pencil an X on top of the handle hoop (pg. 13, #2).
3. Put the two hoops together (pg. 14, #4—#6) except that the top edge of the rim will be placed **below** the line on one side of the handle hoop and the lower edge **above** the line on the other.
4. Weave god's eyes (pg. 29), to bind the two hoops together.
5. The traditional length of all of the primary ribs in a melon basket of any size is equal to half the circumference of a hoop.

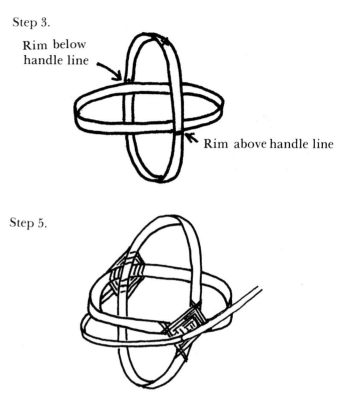

Step 3.

Rim below handle line

Rim above handle line

Step 5.

In this 12" melon basket they will each be approximately 19½" long (10" hoops, 16½" long.) It is a good idea to check before you cut them to see if this length will be correct for your basket. Mark the 19½" (16½") length on a piece of flat oval reed. Hold one end on top of an ear just beneath the basket's rim where it would be if it were already inserted. Hold the 19½" (16½") mark on top of the other ear above where that end will be. The rib should be long enough to curve slightly outward beyond the rim when it is placed in the ears. Adjust the length, if necessary, and cut 6 primary ribs.

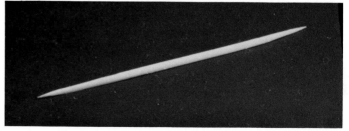

6. Flat oval rib—ends tapered and ready for use.

6. Taper the ribs. Start about 4" from the ends of the flat oval ribs. Use a knife or a small plane and gradually shave each end to a sharp point. Ribs made from round reed may be sharpened with a pencil sharpener.

Step 7.

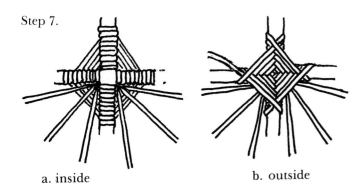

a. inside   b. outside

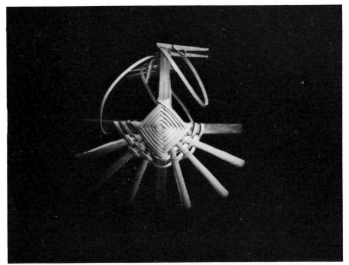

8. Primary ribs in place. First four rows woven.

7. Primary ribs inserted in back of ear.

7. Place the sharpened ends of the ribs in the ears—3 behind each half (a). The ribs may be inserted in the ear reeds to hold them in place, but they should not extend through them to show on the outside (b).

Note: In a traditionally shaped melon basket, the outline made by the ribs looks like the bottom half of a circle. Adjusting the rib lengths so that the basket rests on both the two lowest ribs and the handle base is a variation that will result in a nicely shaped basket and will help to keep the finished basket from rolling to one side.

8. Begin to weave. Remoisten remaining reed ("weaver") from one of the ears. Start at the left of the handle. Bring the weaver under the rim, over rib, etc. (Illus., pg. 20, #12). Weave from rim to rim and back again two times (four rows) or until there is enough room between the primary ribs to insert the secondary ones. Then weave the same number of rows with the weaver from the other ear.

9. Cut, and insert six (3 on each side) secondary ribs in the weaving (pg. 21, #13). These will be about an inch shorter (18½" or 15½") than the primary ones. Sharpen the ends of these round ribs as you would a pencil. Note that the secondary ribs may be placed on either side of the primary ones—whichever fills the spaces better, but each pair of corresponding ribs should be placed the same in both halves of the basket.

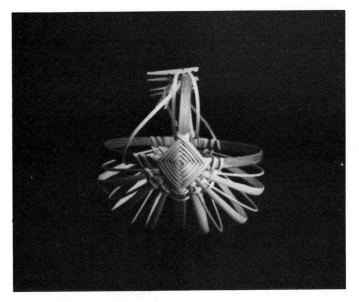

9. Secondary ribs inserted.

10. Continue until the weavers from each side meet and can be overlapped (pg.. 21, #14—#17).

Alternate Rib Lengths for a 10" Basket
Cut 2 each and number each rib for identification (pg. 18, #9)

Primary Ribs	Secondary Ribs
#1 — 16½"	#2 — 14"
#3 — 17½"	#4 — 14½"
#5 — 16½"	#6 — 13½"

The above lengths are only suggestions. Instead of measuring each rib, practice holding the reed in place and cutting them by sight. Change the shape of a basket by varying the lengths of the ribs. Experiment by using flat oval reed for primary ribs; and narrower, flat oval, round, or half round reed for secondary ribs. From North Carolina, basketmaker Patricia Turner suggests using a wide reed for primary ribs, then splitting it lengthwise to make the secondary ones.

Sea grass weavers are fun to work with, and they make a sturdy basket. The grass does not need to be dampened. In fact, soaking it will relax the fibers and cause them to separate. If raveling is a problem, the cut ends of the sea grass may be dipped in glue, or thread may be wound and tied tightly around them.

Combine various types, colors and widths of both natural and commercial materials, and use hoops that are different in shape to create unique patterns and combinations.

8" Roll Basket

8" ROLL BASKET

Materials:
  two 8" carnival hoops (frame)
  #6 round reed (ribs)
  ¼" flat reed (weavers)
Construction:
1. Mark half the circumference of both hoops, with the joint of the hoop that is to be the rim halfway between the rim's two marks. The joint of the other hoop will be cut away and should be at least 2 inches from the marks.
2. Slide the two hoops together, the joint of the vertical hoop above the rim, and mark their positions (pg. 14, #4).

Step 3.

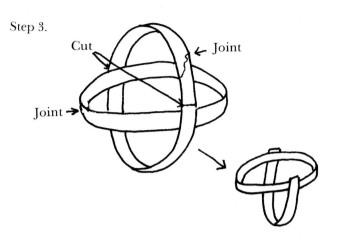

3. Take the hoops apart, and cut off the outside hoop about ⅛" to ¼" above the marks that show the top edge of the rim. Put the hoops back together. The stubs of the outer hoop should extend just high enough above the rim to hold the ear weavers and also round edging reed if a decorative rim is planned.
4. Check to make sure that the two exposed portions of the rim are equal in length, and adjust their positions if necessary.
5. Glue or tie the hoops together (pg. 15, #5 & #6).

Step 6.

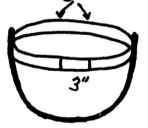

6. Measure the exposed portions of the rim, and mark a 3" space in the middle of each side. i.e. Find the halfway point between the intersections of the two hoops, and draw a light line across the outside of the rim 1½" to the right of this point, and another line 1½" to the left.

Step 7.

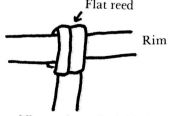

7. Short pieces of flat reed may be folded over the stubs of the center hoop, their ends extending just below the rim. Clip or glue the reed to the hoops. The ears will hold the reed in place and conceal the ends.

Short lengths of reed are folded over the ends of the center hoop. 3 inches is marked in the middle of the rim.

8. Weave three-fold ears (page 16).
9. Cut 6 primary ribs:

Suggested Rib Lengths

Cut 2 each, and number for identification (pg. 18, #9).

Primary Ribs	Secondary Ribs
#1 — 11½"	#2 — 12"
#3 — 13"	#4 — 13"
#5 — 12½"	

10. Follow the general directions for weaving (pg. 18, #10—#17), with the exception that the middles of the rims will be wrapped for handles:

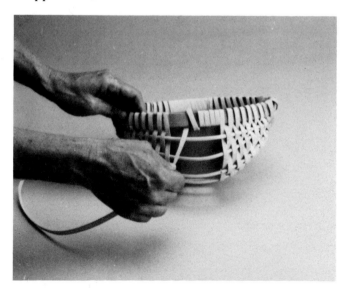

Wrapping the handle.

Step 10a.

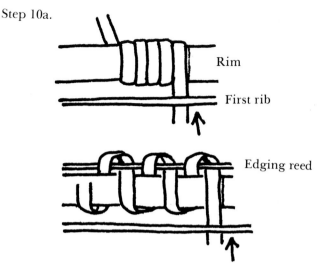

a. When the weaving reaches the first 3" mark on the rim, do not return to the other side. Instead, wrap the weaver tightly around the rim to the second mark before weaving back across the ribs, a. If making a decorative rim, continue between the marks in the established pattern before returning, b.
b. Wrap between the marks as above on the opposite rim with the weaver coming from the other ear. The two weavers will have exchanged places.
c. Finish the basket by weaving only between the first ribs below the rim, reversing around them to return.

Scottish Yarn Basket   (Pictured on page 5.)

Materials:
    Two 12" carnival hoops (frame)
    #6 round reed (ribs)
    ¼" flat reed (weavers)
Construction:
1. Put the hoops together the same as for a melon basket (pg. 38, #3).
2. Mark off a 4" space in the middle of one half of the vertical hoop and another 4" space in the middle of one half of the horizontal hoop for handles (pg. 40, #6). Place the marks on the half of each hoop that does not contain a joint.
3. Weave god's eye ears.
4. Cut 9 primary ribs, 19½" long.

Step 5.

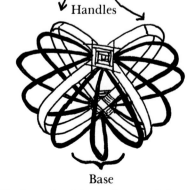

5. Insert 3 ribs in each of 3 quadrants of the ear, leaving the quandrant between the two marked sides open.

6. Weave about 4 rows across all of the ribs and all of the hoops, reversing the weaver to return around the two marked rims.

Note: The weaving will begin at a marked hoop from one ear and at an unmarked hoop from the other.

7. Cut 6 secondary ribs—about 18½" long, and insert them in the weaving. Insert the secondary ribs wherever they will divide the spaces between the primary ribs most evenly, being sure to place each 3 corresponding secondary ribs against the same primary ribs in the different quadrants (pg. 21, #13). The sides of the yarn basket are smoothly rounded like the melon basket, and its rib lengths may be adjusted so the basket will rest on those that fall directly below the middle of the open quadrant.

8. Continue to weave all ribs and hoops until the 4" marks are reached. Then reverse the weavers around the first ribs under the areas marked on the hoops for the handles. Finish the basket by reversing from these ribs instead of the rims.

Note: The handles may be wrapped as in a roll basket (pg. 41, #10).

Potato Basket

12" Potato Basket.

Materials:
One, 12" carnival hoop, ⅝" wide (rim)
#6 round reed (ribs)
¼" flat reed (ears and beginning weaver)
⅜" flat reed (weavers)

Construction:
1. Mark half the circumference of the hoop (pg. 14, #3) with the exception that the marks are drawn inside the rim. *Note: If the handles are going to be wrapped as in a roll basket, the rim joint may be placed in the middle of the sides (pg. 40, #1).*
2. Cut three 21¼" lengths of #6 round reed for the initial ribs. *Note: To determine the lengths of the 3 initial ribs for a potato basket of any size, the following formula may be used: One rib length = ½ the circumference of the rim hoop + 2 times the hoop's width + ½ inch.*

20" Potato Basket. Wide sea grass stripes between "Denim Blue" dyed 1/4" flat reed. Made by Kirsten Gotzsche.

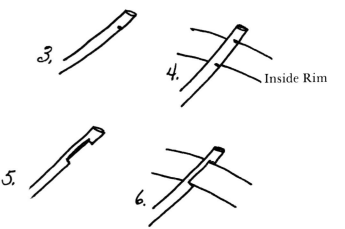

Inside Rim

3. Measure ¼" from both ends of each length, and mark this distance on the *outside curve* of the reed.
4. Hold one of the ribs against the hoop with its mark at the top edge of the hoop, and pencil another line on it at the bottom edge of the hoop. Mark the other end of the rib the same. Repeat with the other two ribs.
5. With a knife, carefully cut a notch between these two lines on all three ribs. Make the notches about one half the thickness of the reed so that the edges of the rim will be partially covered when the reed is fitted against the rim.
6. Place the notched portions of one of the ribs directly over the halfway marks on the inside of the hoop. Glue the hoop and rib together. It is important that these ribs be held firmly in place. They may also be tied to the hoops for a more secure hold.

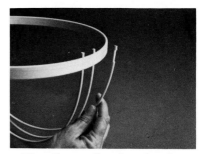

The ribs are fitted to the rim.

Step 7.

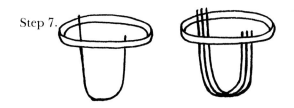

7. Measure 1" to the right and 1" to the left of the ends of the rib, and draw lines on the inside of the rim, then place the remaining two ribs over these lines following the same procedure as with the first.

Step 8.

8. Mark off 4" halfway between each of the two outside ribs on both sides of the rim (pg. 40, #6 with the exception that 2" will be measured from the halfway points instead of 1½").

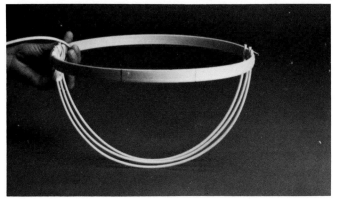

4" for a handle is marked off on the rim. One ear is woven.

9. Select a long (at least 8') length of flat reed, and begin to weave the ears as shown.

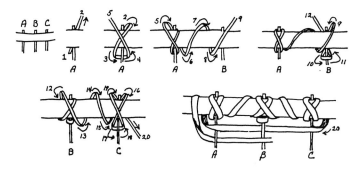

Continue to weave the ear by bringing the weaver over C, under B, over A, around the rim, under A, etc. Keep the rough side of the reed against the rim by giving it a half turn before it is brought up behind it. Turn the reed again as you come from behind the rim so that the smooth side of the reed is again on the outside. Twisting the reed in this manner creates the necessary space for inserting ribs in the ears.

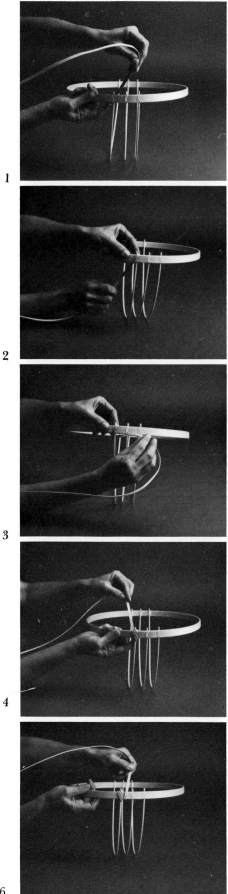

1

2

3

4

5 and 6

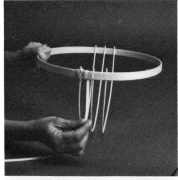

7

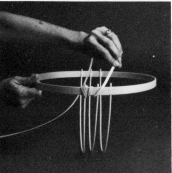

8

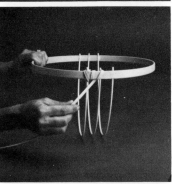

9

10

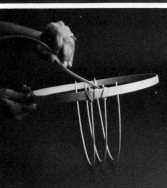

11

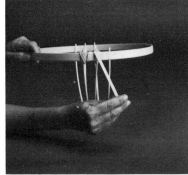

12

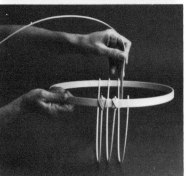

13

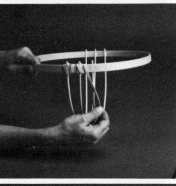

14

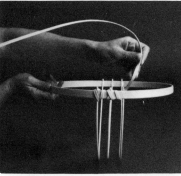

15

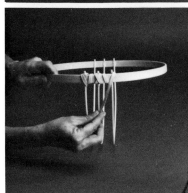

16

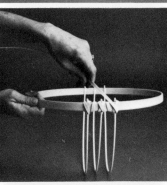

17

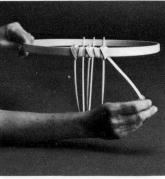

18

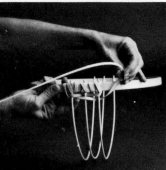

19

20

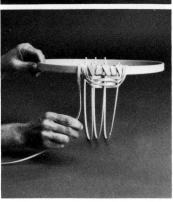

21

10. Suggested Rib Lengths
    Cut two of each, and number for identification.

Primary ribs
#1 — 17"
#2 — 18"
#4 — 19"
#6 — 18½"

Secondary ribs
#3 — 17". Place under #2.
#5 — 17½". Place under #4.

11. Insert the primary ribs.
a. Insert ribs #1 and #2 together in the ears just below the rim. (Since the openings in the ears are small, the diameter of the rib ends should be greatly reduced. Start about 2 inches from the ends, and gradually shave them to a point.)
b. With an awl, pierce the middles of the ears (where the reed crosses) and insert the #4 ribs (pg. 18, #10).
c. Insert the #6 ribs in the ears beside ribs A and C.

12. Insert secondary ribs as needed. *Note: In the basket pictured, increasing was woven on ribs #2, #4 and #6 in the second row from the ear. Secondary ribs were added after the third row was woven. At the beginning of the fourth row, ⅜" reed was added to weave the rest of the basket. The ends of the ⅜" reed were tapered to ¼" and overlapped (pg. 21, #16) with the ¼" weaver. The tapered ends were placed behind the rim on one side of the basket and beneath rib #1 on the other.*

   The remainder of the basket may be worked the same as a roll basket (pg. 41, #10) or as a yarn basket (pg. 42, #8). The handle may also be wrapped after the rest of the basket has been woven.

   In the basket shown, the handle was wrapped with ¼" flat reed after the rest of the weaving had been completed. The beginning end of the ¼" reed was laid against the inside of the handle (rough side of reed out) and was overwrapped about five times to hold it in place. The other end was threaded behind several of the ⅜" weavers on the back of the rim.

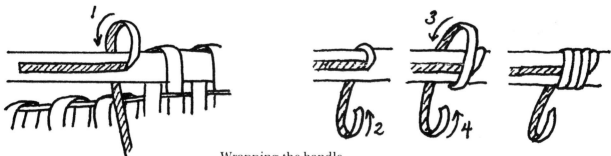

Wrapping the handle.

Egg Baskets. Clockwise from lower left: 3'' basket with 1/8'' weavers made by Eugene Turner, 11'' oval basket with 1/8'' weavers made by author. 10'' basket with #6 round ribs made by Maureen May. 12'' basket with 3/8'' *half round* ribs made by Patricia Turner. Note the different handles.

8'' Egg Basket.

EGG BASKETS

The following instructions are basic to many different kinds of "egg" baskets. Materials can be gathered out-of-doors, found around the house, and purchased commercially. Weavers can be different widths, hoops different sizes and shapes, and ribs curved or bent in different ways. Very small to very large baskets may be woven, and the variety of round, oval and rectangular shapes is limited only by what we are capable of imagining.

This rib basket seems to have about as many names as it has shapes and styles. Many of these names describe how the different baskets were used. The fully rounded woven halves of the traditionally shaped basket kept eggs from rolling against one another when they were gathered or carried to market: hence, an "egg" basket. A deep indentation between the halves enabled one to carry it comfortably against the hip: thus, the "hip" basket; and resting the basket in front of the rider on the neck of a horse or a mule helped to keep it from tipping to one side, a "neck" basket. "Gizzard", "cheek", "butt", and "granny's fanny" are a few of the many derived from the baskets' shapes. An owner's or weaver's name may also identify a particular basket to family or friends. The different names all add greatly to the charm of basketry and often give us an insight into the history of their early owners and weavers.

8" Egg Basket

Materials:

Two, 8" carnival hoops (handle and rim)
#6 round reed (10 ribs)
¼" flat reed (weavers)
Handle length: 12"
Suggested rib lengths:

Primary ribs	Secondary ribs
#1 — 12¾"	#2 — 14"
#3 — 15"	#4 — 14½"
#5 — 13"	

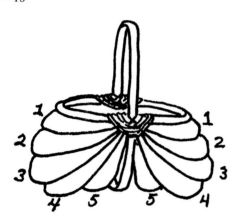

Egg Baskets. Upper left: 10" hoops, 1/2" flat oval primary ribs, woven handle and rim. 8" hoops, 3/8" flat oval ribs. Both baskets made by Patricia Turner. Center: Pincushion. 3" hoops, #4 round reed ribs, "rust" dyed #0 round reed weavers.

Construction:

1. Follow the general directions, pg. 13, steps #1 through 13.
2. Some of the ribs in this basket are considerably longer than others, and it will be necessary to compensate for the differences in length by adding extra rows of weaving to the longer ribs. Now is the time to decide which of the methods for adding this extra weaving you wish to use. See "Compensation", pp. 35-37.
3. Finish weaving the basket, steps #14 through #17 in the general directions, compensating as necessary on the longer ribs.

Many egg baskets rest on ribs #4 and #5. Shorter ribs inserted between each of the #5 ribs and the center hoop will help to maintain the inverted "v" shaped indentation between the two halves of the basket. They may be added with ribs #2 and #4, or at any time during the weaving.

In most egg baskets, inserting just three primary ribs (#1, #3, and #5) in the ears works very well. Add secondary ribs as soon as the weaving leaves enough space between the primary ones to do so (pg. 21, #13). Further ribs can be added at any time, but they must always be added in pairs to keep the weaving even and the basket halves the same.

In some baskets there is room to insert as many as 5 or more primary ribs in the ears:

  a. Insert ribs #1 and #2 together just below the rim, rib #3 in the middle of the ear, and ribs #4 and #5 together beside the handle hoop.

  b. Ribs #1 and #5 may be fastened to the hoops with twist ties or masking tape before the ears are made. The ears will hold them in place, and there will be more room to insert ribs #2 and #4 beside them.

This 16" sea grass egg basket sets on the owner's hearth and is used to store lap robes for cool winter evenings. Made by Kay Grimme.

Suggested measurements for additional sizes: Hoop, handle, and rib measurements are given in inches.

Round reed #	Hoop size	Handle length	Cut two lengths each for ribs.				
			#1	#2	#3	#4	#5
3 or 4	3	4-1/2	5	5-3/4	6	5-1/2	5-1/4
4	4	6	6-1/2	7-1/2	7-3/4	6-3/4	6-1/4
5 or 6	5	7	8-1/2	10	10-1/2	10-1/4	9
6	6	8	9-1/2	11	12	11-1/2	10
6	7	10	12-1/2	14-1/2	15-1/2	15	13
7	10	14	16-1/2	17-1/2	18-1/2	18	17-1/2
7	12	17-1/2	20	23	24-1/2	23-1/2	21
7	14	17	24-1/2	27	30	28	24-1/2
7	16	25	28	31	34	28-3/4	27-1/2
8	18	25-3/4	29	35	41-1/2	38-1/2	31-1/2
8	23	33	37	40	44	40-1/2	39

Variations

10" and 12" Egg Baskets

10" Egg Basket
Suggested materials:
   Two, 10'' carnival hoops (handle and rim)
   ⅜'' half round reed* (primary ribs)
   ¼'' half round reed -or— #6 round reed (secondary ribs)
   Combination(s) of natural or colored ¼" flat reed and #3, or smaller round reed, sea grass, etc. (weavers)
   #6 round reed—optional (woven handle and rim)

12" Egg Basket
   Two, 12'' carnival hoops (handle and rim)
   ½'' flat oval reed* (primary ribs)
   ⅜'' -or— ¼'' half round reed -or— #6 or larger, round reed (secondary ribs)
   ¼'', or wider, flat reed (weavers)
   #6 round reed—optional (woven handle and rim)

   *It is often necessary to re-form the curves of wide reed that is to be used for ribs (pg. 11, ''Ribs'' 7).

16'' sea grass egg baskets. The basket in the foreground is usually filled with large pine cones. Made by Susan Johnson. The basket behind it was made by Kay Grimme.

10" Key Basket

Key baskets were originally used to hold the large keys for locks on various buildings and storage rooms on southern plantations. One side of a key basket curves outward, while the other side is flat so that it may be hung on a wall. The frame consists of an oval handle hoop and a "D" shaped ( ) rim hoop.

10" Key Basket. The handle hoop on this basket is oak. Made by Carolynn Schneider

10" KEY BASKET

Materials:
One, 14" X 10" oval hoop, ¾" to 1" wide (handle)
One, 10" D-shaped hoop, about ¾" wide (rim)
#6 round reed (ribs and rim edging)
¼" flat reed (weavers and ear)
masking tape
needle-nose pliers
Handle length: 20"

Step 1.

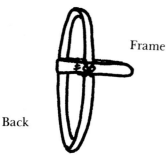

Construction:
1. Put the hoops together. Slide the rim over the outside of the handle with its crosspiece against the handle's edges.

Step 2a.

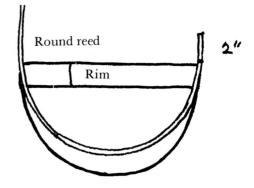

2. Tape round edging reed to the top of the rim: (This decorative reed helps to keep the rim from being pulled downward as the basket is woven.)

a. Lay a long piece of round reed along the top edge of the curved part of the rim with one end of the reed extending about 2" beyond the back crosspiece. Mark where the reed meets the back of the rim. Wet the reed at the marked part only; then soften it further by pinching it firmly with a pair of pliers. Next, bend it carefully to follow the sharp turn of the rim. The reed may tend to splinter, but softening it with the pliers should prevent it from breaking.

b. Hold the reed above the curved front of the rim. Mark where it meets the back of the rim on the other side. Dampen, and bend as before.

c. Cut the reed so that its ends overlap about a half inch.

Step 2d.

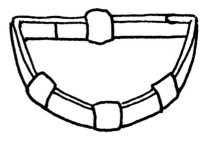

d. Scarf the overlapping ends (pg. 25, diagrams), and tape the reed to the top of the rim with masking tape.

Note: You may wish to get a head start on inserting the ribs by taping those that will be next to the hoops in place. The ears will then be woven over both the ends of these ribs and the edging reed on the rim. Taping the front ribs, #1 and #8, is especially helpful.

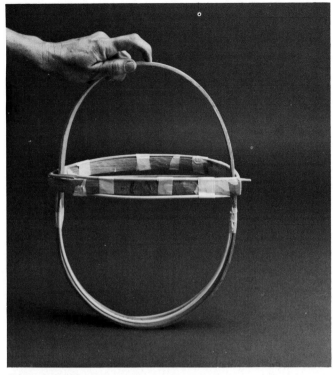

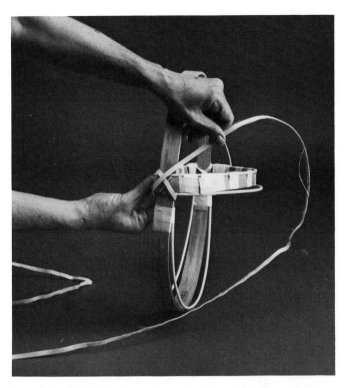

Rim and Ribs #1 and #8 taped.

Starting a 3-fold ear.

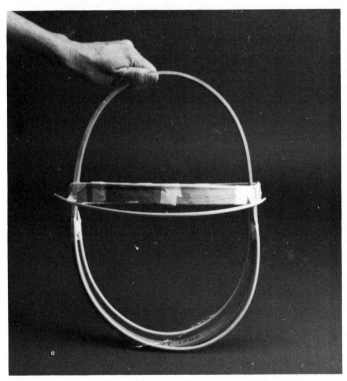

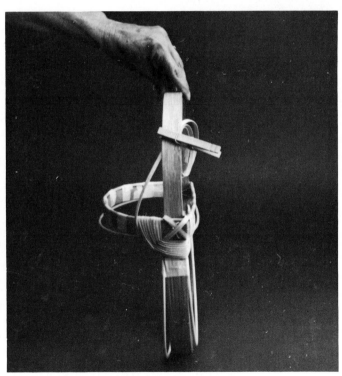

Edging reed and the primary ribs next to the hoops are taped in place.

The ear is woven over the ends of the ribs taped to the hoops and also the edging reed on the rim.

3. Weave the ears. Hold one side of the handle toward you. One half of the ear will be on the curved, front part of the rim; the other half will be on the back, straight part.

4. Cut the ribs, and number or letter each for identification. Be sure to check the suggested lengths by holding the reed in place before cutting it. Directions continue on page 54.

Left: 14" Potato Basket with sea grass weavers. Made by Patricia Turner. Right: Herb Basket. Note double edging reed on the rim. Very narrow weavers are 3/16" flat reed split lengthwise in half. Above: Key Basket with 1/8" weavers.

Antique Key Basket. Even paint can have a patina. This green would be difficult, if not impossible, to duplicate today. The key basket is more of a lowland than mountain basket, but early examples are sometimes found in the highlands. These were probably used as wall baskets for more than just keys. 1/2" handle hoop is 10 1/2" long, but the basket is 15" from top to bottom. Six ribs are placed between the rim and handle base on the back and 7 more ribs extend below the base. 1/2" rim is 9" across the back; the deeply dipping curved front is 19". Twenty-six rounded ribs. 1/2" flat weavers. From the collection of Karen Cauble. Courtesy of "The Cauble House, Folk Art and Antiques", Jamestown, N.C.

Key Basket. Height, 12", width 14". #1 round reed was used for ears and some of the middle rows. Bright pink weavers were overdyed and muted when the finished basket was dyed "antique gray".

Key baskets, large one with lid. Courtesy, The Canery, Winston-Salem, N.C.

Antique Egg Basket, 18" (approx.): Handle and rim widths, 1". Flat weavers are about 3/8". 52 flat ribs vary in width from about 1/4" to 3/4". Finished with gusset in middle of sides. Note the double wrapped rim, and the god's eye which shows English influence in the basket's design. From the Stanton, Virginia area. From the collection of Jim and Cecelia Leonard.

This antique egg basket was purchased in Pennsylvania. The 1/2" wide, uniformly shaped handle is probably hickory, which is seen used more often in baskets from this part of the U.S. than in Southern Appalachia where white oak was more common. The adaptation of familiar designs to more readily available materials provides clues to where people may have lived and the routes that they travelled before finally settling in Appalachia. Handle hoop, 12". Rim hoop, 11". Sixty-four rounded ribs. Weavers near the ear are approximately 1/8", and gradually widening to 1/2" in the center. Note the double wrapped handle. From the collection of Karen Cauble. Courtesy of "The Cauble House, Folk Art and Antiques", Jamestown, N.C.

Primary Ribs
Cut only one of each.

Front	Back
#1 — 13″	A — 9″
#2 — 13½″	D — 12½″
#4 — 15″	F — 17″
#7 — 17″	
#8 — 17½″	

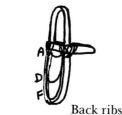

Front ribs   Back ribs

5. Sharpen the rib ends and insert them in the ears:

   a. Insert front ribs, #1 and #2 together, and back rib, A in the ear just below the rim.

   b. Pierce the mid-points of the ears with an awl, and insert front rib, #4 and back rib, D.

   c. Insert front ribs, #7 and #8 together and back rib, F beside the lower handle hoop. The lower curved portion of rib F should come only a short distance from the base of the handle hoop.

Note: If the ears do not allow enough room to insert 2 ribs together, they may be placed in a different sequence, but keep in mind that the total number of secondary ribs added at any one time must always be an even number.

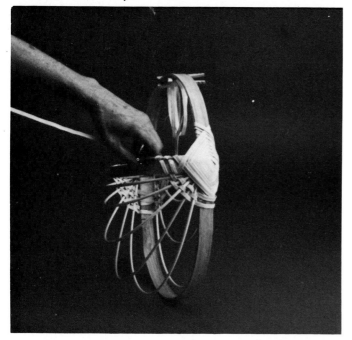

Primary ribs in place.

6. Weave 4 or 5 rows from each ear. The front and back are not woven separately. Weave from rim to rim across all of the ribs just as if the front and back both curved outward.

7. Cut the secondary ribs, checking the suggested lengths before cutting.

Secondary Ribs
Cut only one of each.

Front	Back
#3 — 13½″ place below #2	B — 9½″ place below A
#5 — 14½″ place below #4	C — 9¾″ place above D
#6 — 15½″ place above #7	E — 14½″ place above F

Secondary ribs in place.

8. Weave just enough rows from each ear to hold these secondary ribs in place. Make any adjustments in their lengths that are necessary for the finished basket to be the shape that is planned.

9. Move to the middle of the rim and weave at least 5 rows toward each ear (pg. 22, #18).

10. Return to the sides, and weave until there are about 12 rows from each ear.

11. The back of the basket will fill in first. When no more weavers can be added to its rim, drop down to the rib below it and reverse around that rib to return. When this rib is filled, reverse around the next rib below it, etc. (gusset, pg. 35).

12. Finish the basket by weaving from the sides and compensating by stepping back (pg. 36) on the longer ribs. The side weavers will meet and can be overlapped with those coming from the middle. If there is still room on the longer back ribs, stepping back may be used to fill them, or one or more extra rows of weaving may be added to the lower back ribs at the same time stepping back is begun on the front: Bring the weaver from the front across only the longer back rib(s) before returning. Try to keep from reversing around the same rib in adjoining rows, and reverse around the lowest, longest rib more often than the others.

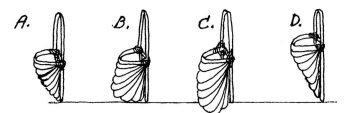

A.   B.   C.   D.

...a few of the possible variations in shape

Alternatives

Key baskets make decorative containers for so many different things that the measurements for the frame and ribs can vary considerably. Decide how long the handle is to be, then tie or glue the rim in place. After the ears have been made, cut the ribs by sight according to the design that is planned. The front can be only slightly curved or fully rounded. The lower rib(s) may rest on the same plane as the base of the handle hoop (A and B) or extend below it (C), or slightly above it (D). Making key baskets in various shapes and sizes will suggest ideas for different ways of weaving them.

A. Other weaving procedures and methods of compensation may be used:

Weave only from the ears, increasing only, and omitting the middle rows.

Combine increasing with a gusset in the middle of both the front and the back.

Use only a gusset on the back and another method or combination of methods on the front.

Fill in on the longer ribs with separate flat or round colored weavers for accent.

B. Key basket frames in the size desired are not always commercially available. Frames of all sizes can be fashioned from honeysuckle vines, grape vines or other natural and manufactured materials. The "D" shaped rim may be placed either over the handle hoop or inside it, although it is usually more secure if it is placed on the outside.

When commercial materials are used, it is easiest to purchase an oval hoop for the handle. Half round reed, narrow oak splint, round reed, etc. can be used to make rims for smaller baskets. For large baskets, sturdy rims can be fashioned from heavy oak splint: Purchase a length of wide white oak splint, and soak it in water until it is pliable. Be patient. If the oak is very dry, it must soak a long time before it can be bent without breaking. It may even be boiled. Curve the splint to form the basket's front, and mark where it will be bent to form the corners of the rim. Score, or cut shallow v's on the rough side. Bend the splint into a "D"—smooth side out. The corners of the D should touch the back edges of the handle. Overlap the ends of the "D" to form the straight, back crosspiece. Shave the ends so that they join smoothly, and staple or use small nails to fasten them together.

This ear, woven along the sides of the handle hoop, compliments the lines of a key basket but offers very little support for the ribs. Much patience is required before they finally are held securely by the weaving. Made by Andrea Neighbors.

7" Key Basket

Materials:

One, 7" X 13" oval hoop—narrow width—about ⅜"
One, 7" D-shaped hoop, about ⅜" wide (rim)
¼", or narrower, flat reed (weavers)
masking tape
needle nose pliers

Handle length: 20"

Ribs: Front ribs, #5, #6, and #7 will extend below the bottom of the handle hoop (pg. 55, example C in diagram).

Front	Back
#1 — 12"	A — 6"
#2 — 13"	B — 6½"
#3 — 14"	C — 7½"
#4 — 14½"	D — 8½"
#5 — 15"	E — 10"
#6 — 14½"	F — 12"
#7 — 14"	

Herb Basket (Pie Carrier)

Materials:
One white oak frame—handle height, about 11½"
   rim diameter, about 10½"
   rim height, 1½" to 2"
#6 round reed (rim edging and ribs)
⅜" flat reed (ears)
3/16" flat reed split in half lengthwise (weavers)

Construction:

1. Cut 2 pieces of round reed, one to lay along the top edge, and one to lay along the bottom edge of the rim. If the handle extends below the bottom of the rim, cut 2 pieces of reed to outline the lower edge. Taper the reed ends and place them against the edges of the handle (pg. 25, #2). This will make a level base for the finished basket.
2. Scarf the rib ends (pg. 25, diagrams).
3. Tape the round reeds to the rim edges, with the scarfed ends at the handle to be covered later by the ears—or overlapping in the middle of the basket to be scarfed and their lengths adjusted later. Place the scarfed ends on opposite sides of the basket.
4. Weave the ears: (The round edging reed is not shown in the illustration.)

Ear

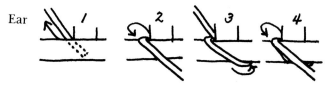

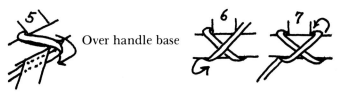

Over handle base

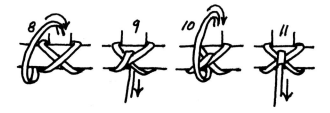

Note: At step 8, bring the reed up in front and down behind the X. Pull the reed tight, covering as much of the existing reed at the lower left as possible. (Make sure the "X" is not pulled downward, but remains centered on the rim.) At step 11, press on the center knot with your thumb to flatten and shape it. Cut off the end of the reed where it emerges from the knot.

10 1/2" x 11 1/2" Herb Basket and 7" x 13" Cradle. Note handles in foot and head of cradle.

Ear Step 1. Place beginning end of the weaver against the outside of the handle.

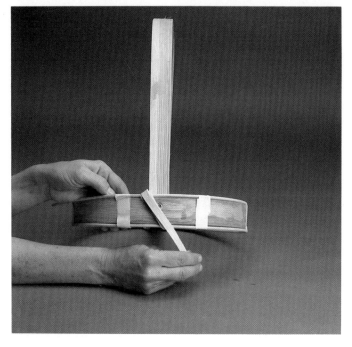

Ear Step 2.

Ear Step 5. Bring the weaver to the inside and across the top of the handle crosspiece.

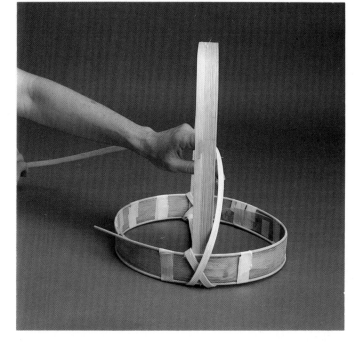

Ear Step 6.

Ear Step 7.

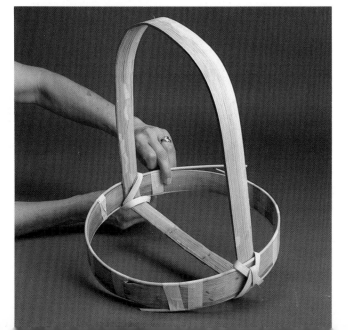

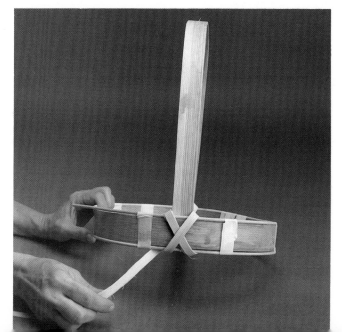

Ear Step 8. Loop the weaver up. Insert it at the "v" made by the intersection of the reed, and pull it down between the reed and the rim. An awl will help to create an opening for the weaver.

Finished ear. The reed has been cut so that its end does not show below the "knot".

Step 5.

5. Cut 6 primary ribs—3 for each side of the handle. The ribs should be cut so that when they are placed in the ears, the open areas on each side of the handle base will be equally divided by them.

Step 5c and d.

Edging reed

Inside rim

Edging reed

#1

#3

#5

a. Cut each length a little longer than needed.
b. Sharpen one end of each of the ribs.
c. With an awl, make 3 holes in the reed in each half of the ears. Pierce the reed in line with the handle's crosspiece so that the crosspiece and ribs will be on the same plane.

Ear Step 11. Flatten and shape the "knot" by pressing on it with your thumb.

d. Insert the pointed end of a rib through a hole far enough for it to touch or lie against the rim.

e. Curve the rib across the bottom of the basket in the desired position. Trim off any excess length and sharpen the other end.

f. Insert the rib through the ear opposite the first as in step d.

6. Weave the base and rim:

Tuck the end of a weaver securely behind an ear.

Weave from the handle toward the rim, beginning by bringing the weaver under rib #5, over #3, etc.

The narrow weaver is 3/16" flat reed that has been sliced lengthwise in half.

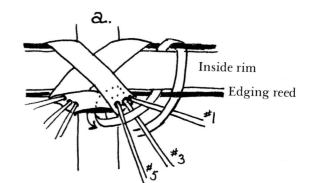

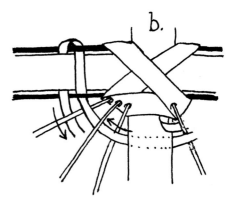

Note: When the weaver comes toward the rim from under rib #1, it should be brought over the edging reed (between the rim and the reed) to the outside, then taken directly against the outside of the rim to the top (diagram a).

When the weaver comes from above rib #1, it should be brought under the edging reed, then back between the rim and reed to the inside and up to the top against the inside of the rim (diagram b). Be careful to keep the edging reed directly beneath the rim. At the top of the rim the weaver is always looped around the edging reed before it is returned to the base. i.e. Bring the weaver between the rim and the reed; loop it around the edging reed, bringing it back between the rim and reed, then down against the side of the rim to the base.

Directions continued on page 62.

Antique Egg Basket, 14'' (approx.). Very unusual fixed half-lid. Two 1/4'' flat ribs are placed close to the lid's crosspiece, and four 1/8'' flat ribs are inserted into the ears. The 14'' x 3/4'' crosspiece has notched ends, which are fitted against the handle, and the woven area of the lid measures 7'' from its outermost curve to the center of the basket. The lid must have been designed for a particular use, but we can only speculate as to its purpose. The handle width is 7/8''. There are 72, approximately 1/8'' flat ribs in the body of the basket. The weaving has been finished with small gussets in the middles of the sides. Of further note are the hand cut square nails that have been used to fasten the rim and handle together. From the collection of Jim and Cecelia Leonard.

The natural contour of a grapevine was the inspiration for this heart-shaped handle. Approximately 14'' x 21''. Made by Andrea Neighbors.

12'' Egg Basket. Oak handle, braided god's eye, 1/2'' flat oval primary ribs. 3'' Egg Basket. 1/8'' flat reed weavers, #4 round reed ribs. Bear made by Chester Freeman.

"My Fat Hen". Much of the extra weaving required to fill the longer ribs in the fully rounded sides of this hen basket was worked with #2 smoked round reed.

Lower left: 10" Egg Basket. Decorative orange reed was woven around the rim after the rest of the basket was woven; primary ribs are 1/2" flat oval. Lower right: 12" Melon Basket. The reed was twisted behind the rim after each row of weaving so that only the smooth sides of the weavers are on the outside. Decorative woven rows were added to the center hoop after the rest of the basket was finished. Primary ribs are 3/8" flat oval. Both baskets made by Patricia Turner. Above: 8" Melon Basket has just six 1/2" flat oval ribs.

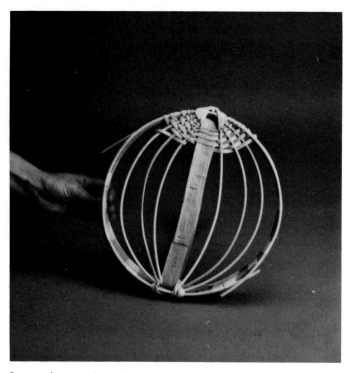

Increasing on the primary ribs.

7. Increasing: Weave only enough rows from each ear to hold the primary ribs in place, then begin to increase on the longer ribs and the rim.

Step 7.

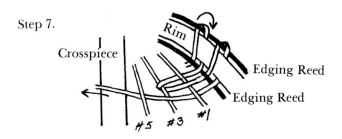

a. When the weaver is returning from the rim, do not weave completely across to the other side. Weave only across the longer ribs. Loop the weaver around a long rib to reverse its direction, and return to weave the rim again before continuing across to the other side of the basket, increasing again on the same ribs and rim.

b. Although the outer ribs and rim require the most weaving, alternate the ribs on which you increase as much as possible. i.e. If you increased to rib #3 on one row, increase only to rib #2 the next time, etc. Since the rim will require the most weaving to cover it, there will be some times when the weaver must be brought around it twice before beginning to weave across the ribs again. It is difficult to judge the number of extra rows that will need to be added to fill the rim, but the closer to the ears they can be placed, the smoother the weaving in the finished basket will look.

8. This basket requires 8 secondary ribs—4 on each side of the handle. They should be added as soon as there is enough space left between them and the primary ribs so the weaving reed can be brought smoothly between them.

9. Continue weaving from the ears, alternately weaving first one side of the basket, then the other, and completing the increasing as early as possible. The weavers from each side will meet and can be overlapped to finish.

Note: If you chose to place the ends of the edging reed in the middle of the rim, stop weaving when you are approximately two inches from them, and scarf the ends (pg. 25, diagrams) while there is still room to do so.

Options:

Make your own frame from oak splints.

If the rim is placed outside of the handle, it should be secured to the handle with staples, small nails, or a very reliable glue.

God's eye, three-fold, or other lashing may be used, but if you intend to set a dish (pie plate) in the basket, make sure the ear leaves enough room to do so.

If the rim comes far enough below the handle base for the basket to set flat, the lower edging reed may be omitted.

If the rim is placed inside the handle, the lower edging reed is a must, or the basket will tip from side to side.

Try using two edging reeds on top of the rim, or omit top edging reed entirely if the rim is high enough without it.

Strips of reed (their ends hidden behind the ears) may be laid against the outside of the rim and woven to make a decorative pattern.

Weaving options for the base:

(see "Compensation", pgs. 35-37)

a. Increase near the ears only.
b. Stop weaving from the ears and weave several rows in the middle of the basket, finishing by stepping back, or by weaving gussets to connect the side and middle weavers.
c. Use a combination of early increasing and a gusset(s).

*Note: If you choose to use a gusset in this basket, it will be worked from the handle base toward the rim. When one side is completed, secure a new weaver under the handle base or a rib and weave the gusset on the other side. It is better **not** to use a single gusset in the middle of this basket as the only method of compensation. There is so much difference in the lengths of the ribs and the rim that large holes would be left in the basket.*

Wide reed may be used for weavers. Start with narrow reed from the ears and gradually broaden to wide (pg. 12, #3).

Hen Basket

Materials:
   one 12'' carnival hoop, narrow width (frame)
   two 8'' carnival hoops, 7/16'' wide (frame)
   ¼'' flat reed (weavers)
   #6 round reed (ribs)
   one 8'' long rectangle of heavy cardboard or light wood
with notches cut ¼'' deep in the middle of each end (brace)

 Brace

Construction:

1. Hold the three hoops together, the large hoop between the two smaller ones and their edges touching at the top. Position the joints at different places on the sides.

Step 2.

12'' Hen Basket. Made by Patricia Henderson.

2. Soak a long ¼'' weaver; fold it in half, and place the tops of the hoops in the fold. One half of the weaver will be on top of the hoops; the other half will be beneath them.

Step 3a.   Step 3b.

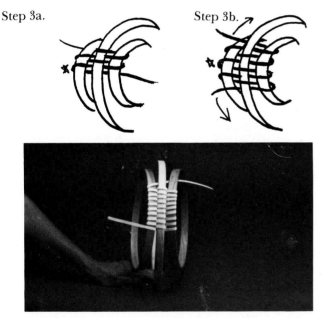

3. Weave the handle, pulling the weaver tight and keeping the hoops as close together as possible.
a. Weave the hoops with one half of the weaver in one direction from the fold (for about 2 inches). Clip the weaver to a hoop to hold it in place.
b. Return to the fold, pick up the other half of the weaver and weave for the same distance in the opposite direction.

8'' hoops are fitted into the notches on the brace.

4. Place your thumbs on top of the middle hoop and your fingers beneath the tops of the outside ones. Slant the 8'' hoops outward by pushing up with your fingers. Place a brace between them, and put the lower inside edges of the hoops in the notches. Make sure the two hoops have the same slant so that both halves of the basket will be alike. These hoops tend to shift out of position until the weaving holds them in place, so it is important to keep checking and re-positioning them until they are secure and the brace can be removed. Directions continue on page 66.

63

The handle and rim were twisted and fashioned into a frame at the same time the grapevine for them was being cut. "Sumac", "Plum" and "wine" colored weavers were over-dyed when the finished basket was dipped in natural walnut stain. Made by Kirsten Goetzsche.

12" Egg Basket. 1/2" flat oval primary ribs, 1/4" flat reed and sea grass weavers, woven handle. Made by Marian Ward.

12" Egg Basket. Primary ribs are 3/8" half round reed. 14" Potato Basket. 1/4" flat reed was trimmed to 1/8" for the first few rows of weaving. Sea grass weavers were used to complete both of these baskets made by Patricia Turner.

The center rib in each of these baskets was cut from a round hoop. Lower left: 8" Combination flat egg and roll basket. Upper left: 5" Roll Basket. Lower right: 12" Potato Basket made by Marian Ward.

Antique rectangular oak market basket. 11" x 16" wide, 8 1/2" high with 12" high oak handle. Rim width, 1". Seventy-two approximately 1/8" rounded ribs. The ribs bend smoothly around the sharp corners, with no splitting of their fibers. Gussets are worked at the corners. From the collection of Karen Cauble. Courtesy of "The Cauble House, Folk Art and Antiques", Jamestown, N.C.

A variety of style. Basket at top made by Patricia Turner.

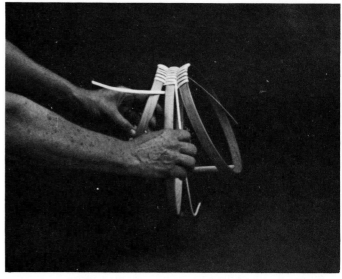

Brace holds small hoops in place as handle continues to be woven.

Inserting the first rib.

5. Continue to weave the hoops in both directions from the top for 1 to 1½", or until the spaces between them are wide enough to insert the primary ribs.

Note: Hen baskets range in shape from ones whose sides curve only slightly to those with sides that are fully rounded. Because of the nature of this basket's design, it is suggested that the ribs be cut by sight (pg. 11, Ribs: #3). The rib lengths which are given here are those of the basket pictured and will be close to, if not the same as, the lengths required for other 12" hen baskets. Mark the suggested length on a piece of reed, and check it by holding the reed in place before cutting the rib.

6. The sooner the ribs can be added, the better, however too little room will cause them to be crowded and the weaving will be bumpy. Before proceeding, see "Alternate rib placement on page 67.

Primary ribs: Cut two of each and number for identification:

$$\#1 — 35''$$
$$\#3 — 31''$$
$$\#5 — 24''$$

Step 7.

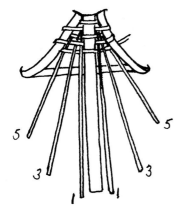

7. Insert the three primary ribs:

a. Insert the #1 ribs through the weaving, next to the center hoop. These ribs should extend about ½" below the hoop so

that both the hoop and the ribs will be on the same plane when the ribs are pulled away from the hoop by the weaving. The basket will rest on these ribs and the center hoop.

b. Insert the ends of ribs #5 alongside the inside edges of the rim hoops. A total of 7 ribs was inserted in each side of this basket. After the secondary ribs have been added, rib #5 will be the third rib from the rim. Check the lengths of these ribs by holding them in the positions they will be after the rest have been inserted (pg. 10, ribs #1).

c. Insert the #3 ribs in the weaving alongside the outside edges of ribs #1. Ribs #3 will eventually be the third ribs out from the center hoop. Check their lengths as with the #5 ribs.

Step 8.

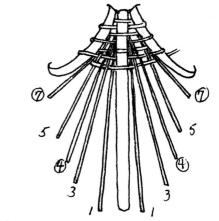

8. Continue weaving for about 1½", or until there is room to add two more ribs to each side of the basket. Insert ribs #4 and #7.

a. #4 — 20" Place next to the outside of rib #3.
b. #7 — 15" Place next to the outside of rib #5.

9. Check the outline made by the ribs, and make any necessary adjustments in their lengths to conform with the shape that is planned for the sides. The sides of this basket tend to flatten while they are being woven. Periodically placing your fist inside the basket and forcing the ribs up and out will help to maintain the curve.

Step 10.

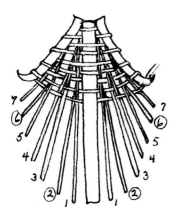

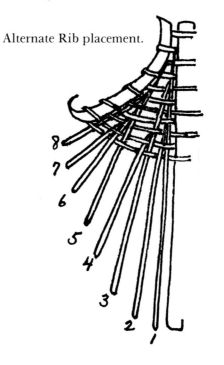

Four Primary ribs were inserted in this basket, and 4 secondary ones have been added.

10. Continue to weave for about 1½" and insert ribs #2 and #6.

    a. #2 — 22" Place next to the outside of rib #1.
    b. #6 — 19" Place next to the outside of rib #5.

11. Continue to weave for about 3 more inches, adding more ribs if necessary. *Note: Early increasing (pg. 35) will help fill the longer ribs in this basket.*

12. After all of the ribs have been inserted and are secure, begin a new weaver at the rim, and weave several rows in the middle of the basket (pg. 22, #18).

13. Finish the weaving by stepping back (pg. 36), working now toward the middle until the weavers meet and can be overlapped.

Alternate Rib placement.

The ribs are numbered consecutively, starting with rib #1 beside the center hoop and progressing to rib #8 at the rim.

1. Insert primary ribs #1 beside the center hoop.
2. Insert primary ribs #5 next to the rim hoop.
3. Weave for 1½", then insert ribs #3 next to the outside edges of ribs #1.
4. Insert ribs #8 next to the outside edges of ribs #5. The #8 ribs should extend about ½" to 1" below the lower edge of the rim.
5. Weave for 1½", then insert ribs #2 next to the outside edges of rib #1.
6. Insert ribs #6 next to the outside edges of rib #5.
7. Weave for 1½", then insert ribs #4 next to the outside edges of ribs #3.
8. Insert ribs #7 next to the outside edges of ribs #6.

Alternate Rib Placement

If the spaces between the hoops are too narrow to insert 3 primary ribs smoothly, only 2 may be used. A different sequence for placing them will be necessary, and there will be a total of 8 ribs in each side of the basket. The lengths of these ribs will be different from those which are given for the basket shown. Cut them to follow the outline planned for the basket's sides (pg. 10, ribs: #1 and #3). See suggested placement which follows.

Oriole Basket

Oriole Basket. Made by Andrea Neighbors.

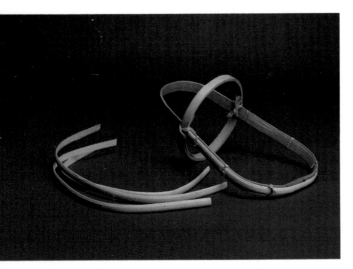

Ribs are shaped around the base of the hoop.

Materials:

    one pre-assembled oriole frame (It will be approximately 6'' X 13'').

    ½'' (or ⅜'') flat oval reed (primary ribs)

    #6 round reed (some primary, and all secondary ribs)

    ¼'' flat reed (weavers)

    Prior to construction of the basket, shape lengths of flat oval for ribs around the base of the handle hoop (pg. 11, #7).

Construction:

1. If the frame is not already nailed or otherwise secured, decide where the rim hoop fits best, and glue or tie the hoops together.

68

Step 2.

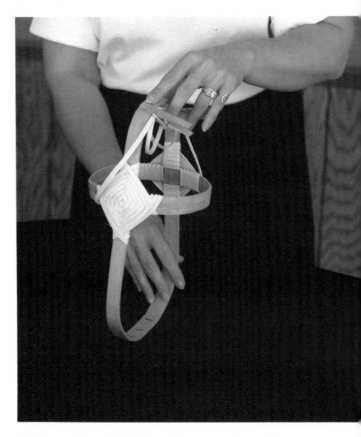

Measure from center of rim

2. Cut 4 flat oval primary ribs: Measure around the base of the handle hoop from the mid-point of where the hoops intersect on one side to the mid-point of their intersection on the other. Subtract one inch to find the primary rib lengths. i.e. If the measurement is 22½'', cut the ribs 21½'' long. (This measurement is for ribs that will be placed in god's eye ears. If a simpler form of lashing is used, longer ribs will probably be required.) Check the lengths by holding the reed in place before cutting. After the basket is woven, it should rest on the 2 lower ribs and the handle base. (The lengths may also be cut so the basket will rest on the handle base and all four of these primary ribs.)

3. Weave the ears: 3-fold, god's eye, etc. depending upon your preference.

4. Start about 2 inches from the ends of each rib and gradually shave them to a point, then insert the ribs in the ears.

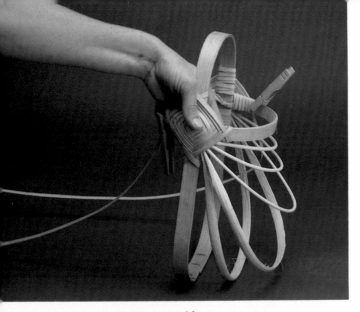

Primary ribs inserted in one side.

Longer primary ribs have been inserted in this basket.

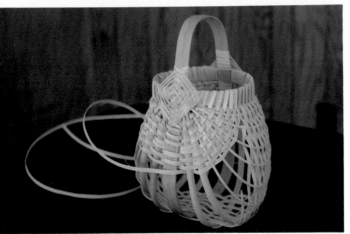

Middle rows woven; weaving continues from the sides.
5. From #6 round reed, cut six more primary ribs by sight (pg. 11, #3) and insert 3 in each half of the ears, placing them to follow the outline that is planned for the basket's shape.
6. Weave the sides, cutting and inserting secondary ribs as necessary. The sides are woven similarly to those of the hen basket (pg. 67, #12 & #13).

Market Basket

MARKET BASKET
Materials:
two 11'' X 14'' rectangular hoops (rim and handle)
½" flat oval reed (ribs #2, #4, & #5)
¼" half round reed (all other ribs)
¼" flat reed (weavers)
optional — #6 round reed (woven handle and rim)
Handle length, 23½"

1. Shape the ribs (pg. 11, #7) at least two days before construction of the basket is to begin:

Step 1.

a. Cut each length longer than suggested below to allow for adjustment when inserted in the basket.

Approximate Rib Lengths
Cut 2 of each and number for identification.

From ½" oval, #2 — 21½" From ¼" half round, #1 — 21½"
#4 — 23¾"   #3 — 23½"
#5 — 20½"

b. Mark the mid-point of each rib, and soak the reed in water until pliable.
c. Find the mid-point of each end of the rectangular hoops, and mark.
d. Lay the flat side of the ribs against the outsides of the hoops, matching the marks. Bend the ribs gently around the corners of the hoops and fasten them in place with twist ties or clips. Let them dry thoroughly before removing.

On the basket that is shown eight additional lengths for ribs were also cut and shaped around the hoops before construction began. As the weaving progressed, it became apparent that further ribs were going to be needed. Lengths were cut for them, and they were fastened to the handle for shaping while the weaving continued on the body of the basket. A total of 24 ribs, 6 flat oval and 18 half round, were used in the basket.

2. Find the mid-points of the sides of the rectangular hoops. Slide the hoops together, handle hoop over the outside of and bisecting the rim. Place the rim below the lines drawn on the sides of the handle hoop.

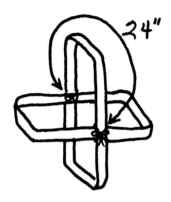

3. Glue the hoops together, tying them also for a more secure hold.

Step 4.   Double wrapping the rim.

4. Optional—Tape #6 round reed to the top edge of the rim and/or the edges of the handle for a woven rim and handle (pg. 24). If a woven rim is not planned, another option is to double wrap the rim.

5. Starting about 4'' from the ends of each rib, shave them gradually to a point.

6. Tape the #1 half round ribs to the lower edge of the rim, and the #5 flat oval ribs to the edges of the handle base. (The ears will be woven over the ends and will hold the ribs in place.)

7. Make traditional ears or any variation which will hold the ribs; however, god's eyes are not recommended since they leave so little room for weaving the handle base and lower ribs. The ears on the basket shown are a combination of two different styles. There were unsightly black stains on the handle hoop, so a braided god's eye was used to cover them. Then the same weaver was used to complete the ear with three-fold lashing.

Step 8.

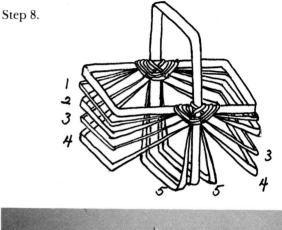

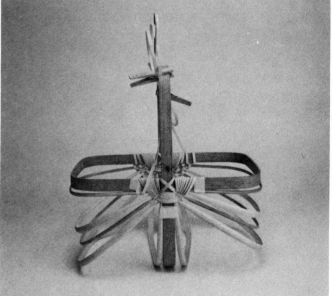

Primary ribs inserted.

8. Moisten the ears, and insert the remaining six primary ribs.

a. Insert the ends of ribs #2 together with ribs #1 in the openings between the ear weavers and the rim. Insert the ends of ribs #4 together with ribs #5.

b. Pierce the dampened ears at their mid-points with an awl, and insert the #3 ribs. Make sure the rib ends are well pointed and dry.

9. Begin weaving the basket with the weaver remaining from the ear, and insert secondary pairs of ribs as soon as there is enough room between the primary ones to do so. Begin to increase (pg. 35, #2) on the longer ribs as close to the ears as possible. Several rows of increasing will need to be woven on

these ribs. Because there is so much difference in the lengths of the ribs, further compensation in the form of gussets (pg. 35, #1) and/or stepping back (pg. 36, #4) may be used as well. Basic increasing was the only form of compensation used in the basket shown.

10. After all of the ribs have been inserted, weaving several rows across the middle of the basket will help retain the basket's shape (pg. 22, #18). Temporary rows, to be removed when it is time to add more ribs, also may be woven across the middle and will help to hold the ribs shaped and in place.

Wedging to keep the ribs shaped.

11. The ribs in this basket tend to curve outward until they are held in place by the weaving. When you are not working on the unfinished basket, wedge it between flat boards, books, etc. to keep it properly shaped. Weights placed inside the basket will help to keep the bottom flat.

Rounded Market Basket. Courtesy, The Canery, Winston-Salem, N.C.

Rounded Market Basket

Follow the same procedure as for making a rectangular market basket. Use two oval, two round hoops, or a combination of each for the handle and rim. When the handle and rim hoops are not alike, the ribs are shaped around the rim hoop. These ribs curve smoothly without the sharp corner bends of those in the rectangular basket.

Classic Appalachian Basket

(Pictured on following page)

Firm weaving across closely placed ribs makes this a strong basket that is admired for both its utility and lovely simplicity of form. The hoops are bound together with simple lashing. Only two primary ribs are placed against the center hoop, and the first weaving is worked from rim to rim across just these two ribs and the hoop. All succeeding ribs are placed next to the last ribs inserted, progressing from the center of the basket toward the rim.

Materials:
    one 12" oak hoop, 1" width (handle)
    one 12" oak hoop ¾" width (rim)
    ½" sturdy flat oval reed (ribs)
    #6 round reed (ribs and rim edging)
    ¼" flat reed (weavers)

Handle length above the rim—18"
Shape the flat oval reed around the hoops prior to construction (pg. 11, #7).

Construction:

1. Tie the hoops together (pg. 13, #1—#6), but do not glue them or cut notches in them to hold the twine.

2. Tape one length of #6 round reed to the top edge of the rim, overlapping its ends 1½" to 2 inches near the middle of a side.

Step 3a.

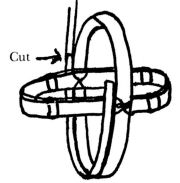

3. Cut the two primary ribs:

a. Lay a long piece of flat oval reed exactly against the edges of the center hoop. Cut the reed long enough for its ends to extend at least 1'' above the round reed on top of the rim. Repeat with a second piece of flat oval reed laid against the other edge of the hoop.

b. Start 9'' from the ends of each rib and shave them very gradually to a sharp point.

Step 4.

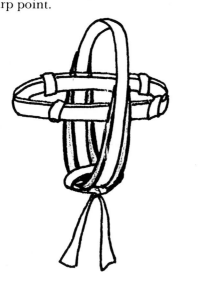

4. Tie the ribs and hoop together at the center of the basket, leaving a ⅛'' space between the edges of the hoop and the ribs. A long, narrow strip of fabric is good to use for tying them.

5. Bind the hoops together over the ends of the ribs:

a. Lay the end of a weaver rough side out near the lower edge of the rim at the left of the handle. Slide it under the rib and insert it between the rim and handle.

b. Twisting the weaver to turn the smooth side of the reed out each time it is to be brought across a hoop, bring it down below the rim and straight across both of the ribs and the handle hoop, then straight up behind the rim and round edging reed returning to the front. Bring the weaver across the ribs and handle just above the rim and round reed, then down behind the back of the rim as shown.

c. Repeat this one time, placing the second row on top of the first.
Classic Appalachian basket, 12'' hoops.

Classic Appalachian. Dogwood frame: Oval handle hoop is approximately 12'' x 17''; round rim hoop, 17''. Stripes woven on the sides were created by using reed that has aged to a darker hue than the other, more recently cut.

Step 5.

Lashing

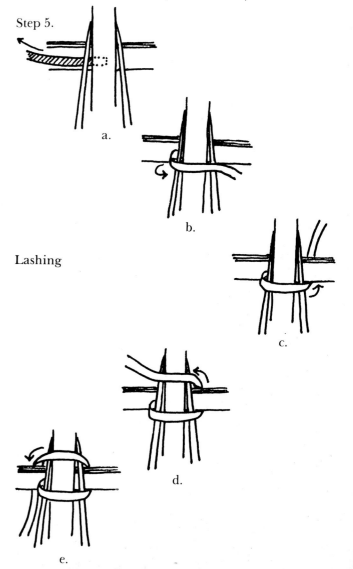

a.

b.

c.

d.

e.

14" Hip, or Neck Basket. This basket rests comfortably against ones hip and is easy to carry even when it is heavily filled. #6 round reed ribs, 1/4" flat reed, sea grass weavers. Made by Carolynn Schneider.

Left: Oriole Basket. Pre-assembled frame, oil base stain. Made by Andrea Neighbors. 12" Melon Basket. 1/2" flat oval primary ribs; #2 smoked round reed used for accent was overdyed when finished basket was dipped in natural walnut stain.

Step 6.

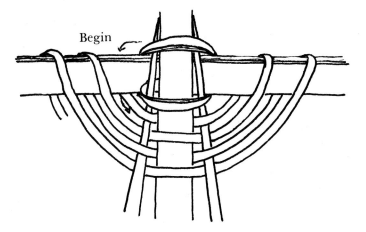

Begin

6. Weave 4 rows from rim to rim on each side of the basket.

Step 7.

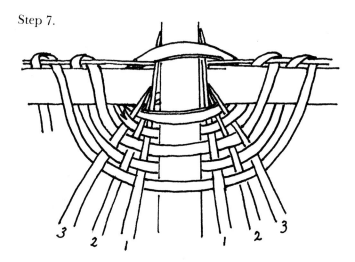

3 2 1 1 2 3

7. Cut four secondary ribs. They will be tied as in Step 4. next to the primary ribs in sets of two, inserting just one rib in each side of the basket at a time. Their edges should exactly follow the outer edges of the ribs they are placed next to just as those of the primary ribs followed the hoop.

a. Start 8'' from just one end of each of the ribs and shave them very gradually to a sharp point. (Both ends may be sharpened if there is no question that the rib length is correct.)

b. Place one secondary rib next to each of the primary ribs: Insert just the sharpened ends through the weaving and under the handle wraps. The ends should lie on the rim against the edges of the primary ribs.

c. Tie all four of the ribs and the hoop together at the center, leaving a ⅛'' space between them. Cut off any excess length from the two uninserted rib ends and shave them to a point as before. Insert these ends through the weaving, positioning them the same as on the rim opposite.

d. Insert the other two secondary ribs the same as the first, except that their ends will lie on the rim against the ends of the first two secondary ribs, and they will not be placed under the handle wraps. Keep the edges of all of the ribs aligned and separated by ⅛'' in the unwoven part of the basket.

All further ribs are added in this way with their ends placed on or just below the rim.

Step 8.

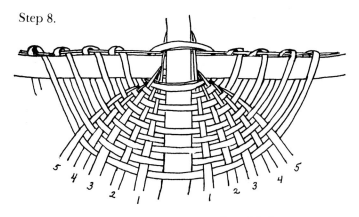

5 4 3 2 1 1 2 3 4 5

Four more rows woven, four more ribs added

8. Weave four more rows and continue by adding four ribs (2 on each side of the basket) after every fourth row of weaving until 7 flat oval ribs have been added to each side.

9. Use round reed instead of flat oval for the rest of the ribs. Continue the pattern, weaving 4 rows and adding 4 round ribs, until the last rib placed is so near the rim that no more ribs are needed. (There are 6 round ribs on each side of the basket shown.)

10. Weave the remainder of the basket, alternately weaving one half and then the other.

11. Stop weaving, and scarf (pg. 25) the ends of the edging reed while there is still room to do so, then continue to weave until the weavers from each half meet and can be overlapped to finish.

Classic white oak basket made by Jesse Jones. From the Museum of Appalachia basket collection, Norris, Tennessee.

Wreath

Materials:

One circular styrofoam form, inside diameter, 12''

¼'' flat reed (weavers)

#7 round reed (ribs)—#6 round reed may be used on smaller wreaths

U-shaped (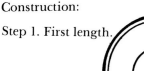) floral pins (to hold ribs in place)

Construction:

Step 1. First length.

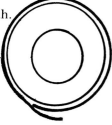

1. Cut the ribs:

1st length—Lay round reed along the outside circumference of the styrofoam form. Cut the reed so that its ends will overlap about 2''.

Step 1. Second length.

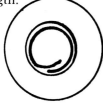

2nd length—Lay round reed along the inside circumference of the form. Cut it so that the ends will overlap as above.

Step 1. Third length.

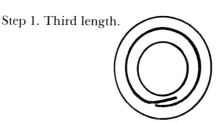

3rd length—Lay round reed on top of the form halfway between the inside and outside circumferences. Cut its ends to overlap as above.

Step 2.

2. Secure the ribs to the form with floral pins, placing the ribs so that their ends are in line with one another.

Step 3.

Start.

3. Begin to weave about 3'' to the right of the rib ends. Insert the beginning end of the weaver under the middle rib. Bring the weaver over the outside rib, and up around the back of the form, then between the inside rib and edge of the form to the front. Pass over the middle rib and go between the form and the outside rib, then around the back, over the inside rib, under the middle rib, etc.

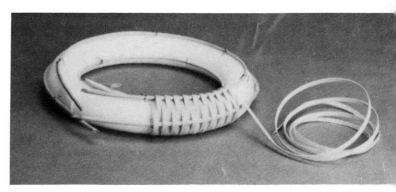

The first rows of the wreath are woven.

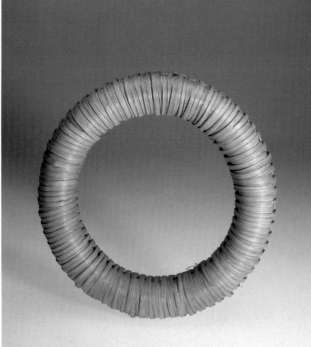

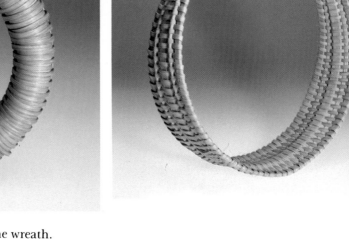

Overlapping weavers on the back of the wreath.

4. Add a new weaver by overlapping it with the old. Conceal the ends of the weavers behind the ribs (pg. 21, #16).

Note: Since the inside circumference of the wreath is smaller than that of the outside, the weaver edges will overlap when they are brought from the back of the wreath to the front. Be consistent in the amount of overlapping that is done each time on the front, and keep most of the overlapping on the back. The weaver edges should just touch each other when the weaver is brought from the front around the outside circumference to the back.

Scarf rib ends

5. Continue around the wreath until the weaving is about 3″ from where the ribs are parted. Stop weaving, and scarf the rib ends. Fit the ends together to make each rib a continuous circle. The scarfed ends may be glued together; however, the final weaving will also hold them in place, and they can be concealed by a bow or other decorations added to the finished wreath.

Materials:
    one 12″ carnival hoop, ¾″ width (frame)
    two 12″ carnival hoops, 7/16″ width (frame)
    ¼″ half round—or sturdy flat oval—reed (ribs)
    ¼″ flat reed (weavers)

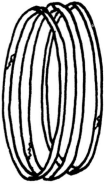

Construction:

1. Hold the 3 hoops together, wide hoop in the middle. Position the hoops so that their joints are on the sides of the frame as far apart from one another as possible.
2. Fold a long weaver around the top of the hoops, and weave them together for 5 inches in each direction from the fold (pg. 63, #2 & #3).
3. Weave 4 more rows in each direction, gradually loosening the weaving to make room for inserting the ribs.

Room to insert the ribs is made by loosening the weaving.
Note: Shelf will be more level is one wider hoop is placed between two narrower ones as in Step 1 under construction.

4. Slant the outside hoops away from the center until just the inside edges of these two hoops rest on the same plane as the center hoop.

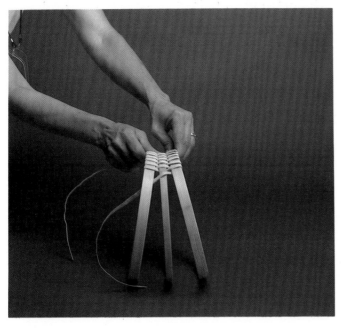

The outside hoops are slanted away from the center.

5. Cut two approximately 32" lengths of half round reed for ribs.

6. Start about 2" from one end of the reed and shave it gradually to a sharp point.

7. Insert one end of a rib in the weaving beside the center hoop. Curve the rib so that it bisects the area between the center and the outside hoops, its lower curve resting on the same plane as theirs.

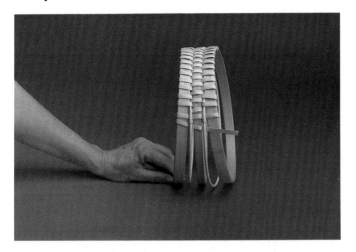

Ribs are inserted in the weaving.

8. Lay the other end of the rib on top of the weavers. Find how far it will reach when it is inserted into the weavers and cut the reed to the correct length. Shave this end as before, and insert it in the weaving beside the middle hoop.

9. Repeat with the second rib, inserting it in the open area between the center hoop and other outside hoop.

10. Continue weaving around the hoops and ribs, periodically checking their positions, until the weavers coming from each direction meet and can be overlapped.

Alternative: The shelf may be widened by taping lengths of #6 or #7 round reed to the outer edges of the outside hoops before beginning to weave. Overlap the ends of the reed near the base close to where the weavers from opposite directions will meet to finish weaving the shelf. The lower curves of these two outside round reed hoops should rest on the same plane as the others. Scarf the ends of the hoops (pg. 25) when the weaving is nearing completion.

Two outside hoops of #6 round reed make a wider shelf.

12" Shelf.

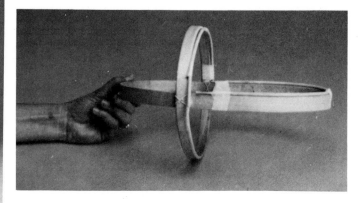

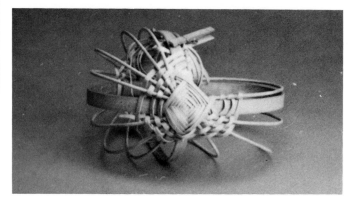

Cradle frame, with round edging reed taped to the bonnet and foot hoops.

Primary ribs in place.

Doll's Cradle

Materials:

    One, 7" round hoop, ¾" wide (bonnet hoop)
    One, 11½" X 8" oval hoop, ¾" wide (rim)
    ¼" flat reed (weavers)
    #6 round reed (ribs)

Construction:

1. Mark half the circumference of the bonnet hoop—about 11½". (See rim hoop, pg. 14, #3) Lightly pencil an X on top of the hoop.

Step 2.

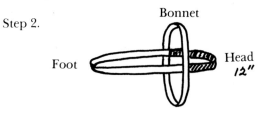

2. Divide the rim hoop in half lengthwise, and mark. Measure 6" in each direction from the mark at one of its ends. This portion will be the head of the cradle. The remainder will be the foot. Take note of the splice where the rim hoop has been glued together. It may be placed in either the head or the foot.

3. Put the hoops together, pg. 14, #4, with the exceptions noted below.

    a. Place the top edge of the rim just **below** the line on one side of the bonnet hoop, and the lower edge just **above** the line on the other side.

    b. Place the bonnet hoop to the **left** of the line on one side of the rim and to the **right** on the other.

4. Glue, or tie the hoops together. Optional: Tape decorative edging reed to the foot and bonnet rims. Primary ribs which border the hoops may also be taped in place at this time (pg. 50, Note).

5. Weave god's eye ears (pg. 29)—7 or 8 wraps.

6. Cut 3 sets of primary ribs and carefully number or letter each for identification. Check the ribs by holding them in place and adjust their lengths to compensate for any differences in hoop measurements.

Suggested lengths. Cut one of each.

Bonnet	Head	Foot
A — 10¾"	1 — 12"	II — 18½"
C — 11½"	3 — 12"	IV — 18"
E — 12"	5 — 11"	VII — 12"
F — 11½" (optional)		

This sequence of rib placement may be altered. Some of the secondary ribs may be changed to primary ones, or fewer secondary ribs may be inserted and additional ones added later. Keep in mind that the number of secondary ribs added to the weaving at any one time must be an even number.

Step 7.

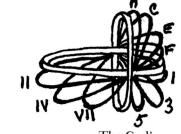

The God's eye is not shown

7. Insert the primary ribs in the ears as follows:
Head: 1, 5, 3   Foot: II, VII, IV   Bonnets: A, (F), C, E

8. Begin to weave with the weaver remaining from an ear. The first ribs woven on one side will be those in the foot. The first ribs woven on the other side will be those in the head. Continue across all ribs and hoops in the foot, head, and bonnet. Bring the weaver around the bonnet or foot hoops to return. (You may wish to trim the weaver to a narrower width for the first few rows (pg. 12, #3).

9. Weave 5 rows, or as many as are needed to hold the ribs in place and to make room for secondary ribs.

Step 10.

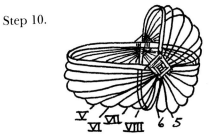

10. Cut, and insert the secondary ribs. This basket will rest ("rock") on ribs V, VI, VII, VIII, hoop 6 and 5.

Suggested lengths:

Bonnet	place
B — 9''	above C
D — 10½''	'' E

Head	place
2 — 10''	below 1
4 — 10''	'' 3
6 — 9½''	'' 5

Foot	place
I — 15½''	above II
III — 16''	'' IV
V — 13¼''	below IV
VI — 11¾''	above VII
VIII — 9½''	below VII

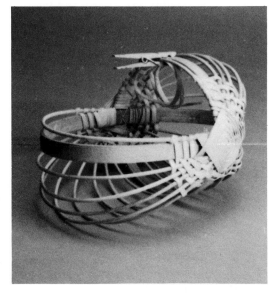

Secondary ribs in place.

Rows of weaving across the middle of the basket.

11. Check the outline formed by the ribs to make sure the cradle will be the desired shape. Adjust the rib lengths if necessary.

12. As soon as the secondary ribs are held securely, move to the middle of the basket and weave several rows toward each ear (pg. 22, #18). If more secondary ribs are to be added later, a few temporary rows may be woven to help hold the basket's shape.

13. Finish by weaving from the ears, compensating as necessary to fill the longer ribs, until the weavers coming from opposite directions meet and can be overlapped.

There was no commercially made round hoop that would fit the odd size oval hoop used for the basket shown on page 80, so a bonnet hoop was made from a length of flat oval reed. All of the ribs were inserted in the ears at the beginning, and no secondary ribs were added. Early increasing was the only method of compensation used.

A round hoop may be constructed as follows:
1. Cut one length of ⅝'' flat oval reed 1¼'' longer than the desired circumference of the finished hoop.

Step 2.

Shave

2. Shave the bottom of one end and the top of the other for 1¼'' so that when they are overlapped, they will be the same thickness as the rest of the hoop.

3. Overlap the shaved ends to form a round hoop, and glue them together.

Steps 4 and 5.

4. Further strengthen the bond by cutting 3 small notches along each side of the glued portion.

5. Place waxed thread or dental floss in the notches, and securely tie the hoops.

6. When the hoops are put together, position the glued and tied portion of the bonnet hoop just below the rim. It will be covered and hidden by a god's eye.

Oriole Basket. There are eleven ribs on each side of the basket.

12'' Wreath made by Patricia Turner.

Cradle. A bonnet hoop to fit the odd size oval hoop of this basket was made from white oak splint.